LOCAL ELECTIONS AND THE POLITICS
OF SMALL-SCALE DEMOCRACY

LOCAL ELECTIONS AND THE POLITICS OF SMALL-SCALE DEMOCRACY

J. Eric Oliver

with

Shang E. Ha and Zachary Callen

PRINCETON UNIVERSITY PRESS
PRINCETON AND OXFORD

Copyright © 2012 by Princeton University Press
Published by Princeton University Press, 41 William Street,
Princeton, New Jersey 08540
In the United Kingdom: Princeton University Press, 6 Oxford Street,
Woodstock, Oxfordshire OX20 1TW
press.princeton.edu

Library of Congress Cataloging-in-Publication Data

Oliver, J. Eric, 1966–
Local elections and the politics of small-scale democracy / J. Eric Oliver with
Shang E. Ha and Zachary Callen.
       p.   cm.
Includes bibliographical references and index.
 ISBN 978-0-691-14355-2 (hardcover : alk. paper)—ISBN 978-0-691-14356-9
(pbk. : alk. paper)
1. Local elections—United States. 2. Democracy—United States. I. Ha, Shang E.
II. Callen, Zachary. III. Title.
JS395.O55 2012
324.60973—dc23   2011051379

British Library Cataloging-in-Publication Data is available

This book has been composed in Sabon

Printed on acid-free paper. ∞

Printed in the United States of America

10   9   8   7   6   5   4   3   2   1

For Raymond E. Wolfinger,
a great teacher, mentor, and friend

Contents

Acknowledgments

THIS BOOK OWES its existence largely to the support and encouragement of a number of individuals and institutions. We are greatly indebted to feedback from Sarah Anzia, Michael Bailey, Adam Berinsky, John Brehm, Jake Bowers, Andrea Campbell, Jamie Druckman, Brian Gaines, Daniel Hopkins, James Kuklinski, Paul Lewis, Paul Peterson, Robert Putnam, Tom Rudolph, Betsy Sinclair, and Cara Wong. Earlier versions of this work were presented at Harvard, Georgetown, and the University of Chicago, and we are grateful to these institutions for providing support of this work. We are especially grateful to Chris Berry, Elizabeth Gerber, William Howell, and Jessica Trounstine, who were incredibly generous in sharing data, time, and attention to this project. Matt Muttino and Ben Oren also provided outstanding research assistance. This research was financially supported by a Young Investigators CAREER grant from the National Science Foundation and by additional research support from the University of Chicago.

LOCAL ELECTIONS AND THE POLITICS
OF SMALL-SCALE DEMOCRACY

INTRODUCTION

WHO GOVERNS AMERICA?

Many people would say the United States is ruled by the president—as the single office selected by all Americans and the head of the executive branch, the presidency commands more power than any other elected position in the land. Others might say that America is governed by Congress—with its ability to pass legislation, approve executive and judicial appointments, and exercise the "power of the purse," Congress ultimately wields the upper hand in any political contest. Still others point to big corporations, unions, and other special-interest groups like the National Rifle Association (NRA) or the American Association of Retired Persons (AARP).[1] These groups "govern" America not only through the direct lobbying of the various branches of government, but also in their ability to shape elections. Because candidates for congress and the presidency are so dependent on the efforts and campaign contributions of such interest groups, they repeatedly bow to their preferences.

This debate is probably familiar to most readers. It has animated American political discourse since the writing of the Federalist Papers. It speaks to fundamental concerns over the distribution of power and popular governance. It dominates the coverage of politics in the popular media. And its focus on national politics encapsulates the way most people conceptualize American governance. But this debate also suffers from a major problem—it overlooks an enormous part of America's governing structure.

Outside of Washington, there exists a largely unrecognized political entity that exerts an enormous influence on American society. It accounts for over $1.6 *trillion* in spending every year, roughly a quarter of the nation's gross domestic product. It collects more

---

[1] The amount of political writings on this topic are too numerous to document, but some recent notable examples include Bartels 2008, Hacker and Pierson 2010, and Frank 2004.

revenue than the federal government does in income taxes.[2] And, arguably, its daily decisions have a more direct impact on Americans than most of the laws and regulations made in Washington, D.C. It tells us where we can live, how we can dress, what we can eat, and how we can act in both public and private places.[3]

This political behemoth is local government and if we want to know "who governs" America, then we need to look beyond the forces that shape national politics and include the factors that influence local politics as well, particularly local elections. In doing this, however, we run into an immediate problem: we know comparatively little about local government and electoral politics in the United States. The overwhelming majority of people who make their living studying politics, such as political scientists, pollsters, pundits, and journalists, focus mostly on national elections. Rarely do they pay much attention to local contests. In fact, over the past fifty years, nearly *all* the published scientific research on American electoral behavior has focused on presidential or congressional races.[4]

Although these experts have developed very good models of presidential and congressional elections, their explanations are actually ill suited for explaining local voting behavior.[5] National elections tend to hinge on partisan loyalties, candidate charisma, retrospective evaluations of economic conditions, and voters' stances on a few key issues. These factors are of limited applicability to local elections for several reasons: most are nonparti-

---

[2] This does not include payroll deductions for Social Security and Medicare.

[3] If one thinks such a statement is hyperbole, consider just the zoning ordinances, liquor and food regulations, and public decency laws that are enforced by most municipalities.

[4] Berry and Howell (2007) estimate that fewer than 1 percent of articles on voting behavior in the top political science journals between 1980 and 2000 were on local voting.

[5] Not only do we know who is likely to win the presidency months before an election, we can also predict, with a better than 90 percent accuracy rate, how any individual is likely to vote based on just four pieces of information. Looking at cumulative data from the American National Election Studies, we find that a two-party model of vote choice correctly predicts 92 percent of variance in voter behavior where the dependent variable is support for the Democratic candidate, and the explanatory variables are a five-point party identification scale, a combined feeling thermometer for the Democratic and Republican candidates, a retrospective evaluation of the economy over the preceding year, and stances on abortion and on spending for the environment and foreign aid.

san; the criteria for judging incumbents' performance are unclear; contentious issues are often hard to identify; and, unlike national contests, we don't have much of an understanding about what voters actually know about local candidates and issues. Most explanations of national voting not only are inappropriate for most local elections but also cannot account for why so many are uncontested, explain what drives evaluations of incumbents, or simply define the broader contours of local politics. While we may know a lot about how and why people vote for president, when it comes to explaining why Jane Smith beat Frank Jones for local supervisor, the best that most voting experts can offer is mere speculation.

Unfortunately, the few existing studies of local elections are not very helpful either because they focus almost exclusively on voting in large cities. Indeed, most of what we know about local politics comes from the study of New York, New Haven, Atlanta, Chicago, Los Angeles, and a few other cities; meanwhile most Americans live in places that are much different from these big, urban centers. As illustrated in figure I.1, three in four Americans live in a community under 100,000 in size.[6] Few of these places have the racial and economic diversity of a New York or Los Angeles. Few have their own airports, convention centers, public housing, newspapers, television stations, or hospitals. Nor do they typically have the corporate headquarters or large-scale business enterprises found in bigger cities. Given these differences, elections in Atlanta, Chicago, or Los Angeles will be more the exception than the typical case of local politics in America. In short, if we want to understand "who governs" America, we need to consider electoral politics in the smaller towns and cities where a majority of Americans actually reside.

This, however, presents us with a very big challenge—how do we compare the nearly 90,000 local governments that exist in the United States? America is not just differentiated by national and

[6] Given the large number of "suburbs" with populations over 100,000, these figures actually inflate the percent of Americans living in "cities" as most people traditionally think of them.

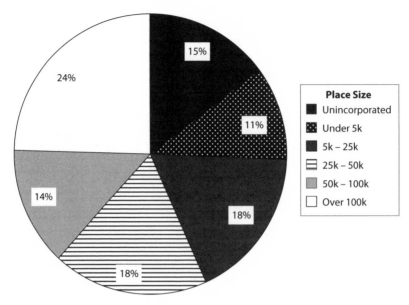

Figure I.1. Distribution of the American population by place size. *Source*: 2000 U.S. Census, STF3C.

local governments or even by big cities and small towns, but by a plethora of smaller local municipalities, counties, school districts, and other special district governments. These smaller governments exhibit an incredible diversity in their size, economic and social composition, and civic and political institutions, a diversity that should also affect their local politics. One would expect that elections in affluent Malibu, California should be very different from gritty, industrial Riverdale, Illinois or bucolic Brenham, Texas. But how can we compare places that are so distinct without getting lost in each of their peculiarities? How can we identify "who governs" America when Americans live in so many types of places and under so many types of government? This book seeks to provide an answer.

We start this inquiry by first stepping back and viewing local politics through a wide conceptual lens. Before we can understand local elections, we need to identify what characteristics differentiate local governments from national governments and from one another. In other words, among the entire universe of democratic governments, including nations, states, counties, municipalities, and special districts, what are the traits that are most important for distinguishing them from each other and shaping their politics? In chapter 1, we identify three such traits: *size*, *scope*, and *bias*. If we were to compare all the democratic governments in the world, we can predict a lot about voters, candidates, campaigns, and the dynamics of vote choice if we know how many constituents they have (their *size*), how much power is in their offices (their *scope*), and how evenly they distribute their resources among their members (their *bias*). Electoral politics are much different in larger democracies than smaller ones, in broad-ranging institutions than narrow ones, and in democracies that direct resources to particular groups rather than those that distribute them universally.

Where a democracy resides on each of these three dimensions will determine whether ideological or civic-minded politicians run for office; whether citizens are mobilized to vote by racial appeals, financial incentives, or civic duty; and whether voters will base their decisions on issues, candidate charisma, partisanship, or other factors. Larger democracies, for instance, simply by having more people in them, are also more likely to have more potential candidates with the ambition or drive to seek leadership posts. Democracies that have greater scope are likely to foster more ideologically motivated candidates and parties. And, as democracies become more biased, their elections become more "partisan" in the sense that there are now groups who are divided in a zero-sum competition over collective resources. Not only can *size*, *scope*, and *bias* explain the political differences between the nations of Bermuda and Botswana or between the nation of India and the town of Ipswich, but also among the town of Riverdale, the county of Riverside, and the Rosewood School District.

With this theoretical framework in hand, we can then turn our attention back to the question of "who governs" and what differentiates the electoral politics of municipalities under 100,000 in size, what will henceforth be known as *local* governments.[7]

---

[7] It is important to recognize this definition of local government as distinct from "urban" government, which I would define as any place above 100,000 in population size.

Because of their differences in *size*, *scope*, and *bias*, the factors that shape electoral politics in most local elections are very different than those in presidential, state, or even big city contests. The United States, for example, is a country high in size, scope, and bias. Its elections are massive undertakings, involving tens of millions of citizens voting for offices with nearly unlimited powers and for stakes that are highly differentiated across the population (i.e., interest groups like senior citizens and farmers get a disproportionately high level of federal revenue compared to most average Americans). These characteristics are manifest in the country's electoral politics: most voters base their choices on general heuristics like party or candidate charisma; parties and candidates are divided by enduring ideological and economic cleavages; and elections are fiercely contested by an array of interest groups seeking to expand or protect their privileges.

Local elections, by contrast, are more intimate affairs usually involving less than a few thousand voters deciding on offices with limited powers and for stakes that are often undifferentiated for an entire constituency (i.e., most residents in a town, for example, get relatively equal levels of fire and police protection). The remainder of the book examines how these differences influence the character of local electoral politics. Through a combination of case studies, national surveys, aggregate statistics, a study of Chicago-area politicians, and a unique survey of voters in thirty localities, we will examine how the *size*, *scope*, and *bias* of America's municipalities influences who turns out in local elections (chapter 2), who runs for local office (chapter 3), when and why local incumbents win or lose (chapter 4), and what shapes individual vote choice (chapter 5). Together, these empirical chapters will show how local elections differ both in regard to national elections and among each other.

The primary difference between national and local elections is that while the former are highly ideological, the latter are *managerial* in character. In a "managerial democracy" electoral politics

---

Thus while the study of local politics typically focuses on the politics of big cities, for the purposes of this book "local" will refer to those smaller municipalities that are typically overlooked.

are primarily about the custodial performance of incumbent regimes. When Americans vote for a mayor, city council member, or association officer with few powers and a limited jurisdiction, their electoral behavior primarily will be a referendum on that person's managerial competence (or guesses about his or her future managerial competence). In most circumstances, incumbents will be successful if they simply maintain a preexisting equilibrium between taxes and services and if they can avoid major scandals or faux pas. This seemingly low bar of performance is attributable to the nature of elected office in most managerial democracies, which consists of little or no pay, demanding work, and limited opportunities for major initiatives. Not surprisingly, incumbents in managerial democracies often run unopposed and enjoy high rates of reelection.

Unlike national offices, the politics of local governments are rarely fought along ideological lines. Whereas debates among "liberal" and "conservative" elites dominate national and state politics, most local governments are not amenable venues for contesting liberal, conservative, or any other ideological visions of social organization. Most American towns do not sustain the chronic political cleavages of states or the country, partly because losing sides to any political battle can easily "exit." In other words, a conservative voter can easily move out of a liberal town, a disaffected community can seek to secede from a larger city, and so on. This is not to suggest that major political or ideological conflict will never emerge in all localities; rather, such struggles are likely to be more of an exception than the rule.

When political conflict does arise in most local governments, it will typically be over issues that are parochial and temporal in nature. Although local politics tend to focus on broad issues of land and economic development, the specific issues that animate local politics are likely to be particular to a certain place and time. For instance, a town may be divided over a proposal to build a new shopping center, but this same fight is unlikely to be found across all towns or even in the same place five years down the road. The parochial nature of small-scale democracy, however, does not mean that local politics are meaningless or shallow. One of the most common misperceptions about local politics is that, in the absence of traditional ideological conflict, their issues are insignificant and that voters are apolitical. In fact, just the opposite is more often true—local voters are much more likely to embody the classical notions of an informed and rational *polis* than are national voters.

This paradox is largely attributable to the selective differences in electoral participation. Local elections are populated largely by long-term residents and homeowners, what economist William Fischel (2005) has elegantly termed "homevoters." Not only are "homevoters" much more likely to vote, they are also better informed and more engaged in local politics than the average voter in national elections. Because of this, contested local elections are less likely to be decided by general heuristics like party affiliation or candidate attractiveness—the mental shortcuts that drive voting behavior in most national or state contests. Instead, as previously noted, they tend to revolve around managerial performance or issues specific to a particular place and time. In short, when issues and conflict do arise in local elections, they are likely to be decisive in local politics precisely because of the types of people who turn out to vote.

Ironically, the highly engaged nature of the local *polis* also makes it exceedingly difficult to predict when and where specific issues are likely to emerge in an election and how they will get translated into particular voting behaviors. Unlike national elections, which are defined by long-standing political cleavages, local politics, for a variety of reasons, have fewer chronic issues that divide the citizenry. The absence of perpetual conflict often may give the appearance of political tranquility, but it masks the latent potential for political furor. Because citizens' local political involvement is predicated so highly on strong emotional attachments to their communities, a political firestorm can be triggered by what may seem to be the most trivial of causes, particularly to an outsider. A mayor may suddenly face a challenger because of a decision to cut down a particular tree or a city council member may lose reelection for making an off-handed remark about a particular constituent. Then again, they may not. The difficulty for both locally elected officials (and those of us who seek to understand local elections) is that it is very hard to know when such a decisive event will arise. Like volcanic eruptions, local politics tends to be dominated by periods of general calm that are occasionally, and seemingly randomly, punctuated by intense tumult.

In addition to identifying what differentiates national and local elections, our empirical investigations also reveal differences among local elections, many of which are attributable to variation in their relative *size*, *scope*, and *bias*. Although local governments are relatively similar in each of these dimensions, especially compared to national governments, they are not identical in these ways. America's municipal governments can hold eight citizens or eight million; they can provide a wide range of public services or few; they can be rife with political patronage and favoritism or be governed in a universalistic manner. These distinctions have important political consequences. For example, elections in larger places involve more ambitious candidates and large-scale mobilization efforts, while voters in smaller places are more likely to know candidates personally and base their votes on this knowledge. Incumbents in towns that provide more government services are more vulnerable than those in municipalities that provide fewer government services, a by-product of their greater scope. Similarly, elections in poor communities (which tend to be more biased) are more fiercely contested than elections in wealthy places (which tend to be less biased).

Together these findings call into question the common characterization of local politics as being dominated by propertied elites preoccupied with economic development; rather, it is more appropriate to characterize local politics as being dominated by propertied masses. To appreciate this point, it is important to consider how we understand local government. Ironically, the question of "who governs?" used to be asked primarily in relation to local politics (Dahl 1961). Fifty years ago, scholars fiercely debated whether America's local democratic institutions allowed for meaningful self-governance or whether they were simply another device used by the affluent and propertied classes to uphold their economic and social privileges. However, when looking at the entirety of American localities through the conceptual lens of *size*, *scope*, and *bias*, it is clear that most theories about community power that arose from these debates are suitable only for a handful of large, urban cities. Although property development and environmental considerations are almost always the central preoccupations of local politics, in most places there is not a rapacious "growth machine" (e.g., Logan and Molotch 1987) setting the municipal agenda. Nor do most places witness shifting constellations of various political interests trying to come together in a "governing regime" to accomplish major public works (Stone 1989). Rather, the political terrain of most American localities is defined by the concerns of local stakeholders with the quality of their living environments, the maintaining of property values, and the balance between low taxes and basic service provision. The small size, limited scope, and low bias of most places greatly attenuate most of the political cleavages that fracture large, urban places.

Viewed through the lens of size, scope, and bias, we can also appreciate why local governments are not effective venues for redressing most deep social or economic cleavages. Although political activists across the ideological spectrum often look to local grassroots action as a vehicle for empowerment, the narrow scope and low bias of most local democracies greatly inhibit the pursuit of any ideologically driven goals. While an activist city council may pass the occasional ordinance against global warming or seek to ban books on evolution from public libraries, the main expenditures and tasks of local governance (e.g., fire and police protection, water and waste management, zoning and street maintenance) simply do not leave a great deal of discretionary resources or leeway for advancing a broader social agenda, particularly in regard to larger visions about the scope of government in society.

Given that dominant theories about local politics seem ill-suited for explaining the electoral dynamics of most American localities, what can we say about the perennial question of "who governs?" Although this book does not provide any simple answers, it does provide a framework for the reader to reconsider this question from a new perspective. In other words, by reexamining local government in terms of their *size*, *scope*, and *bias*, we can restate the question of "who governs" as a question of how does changing the size, scope, or bias of a small-scale democracy affect the ability of its citizens to govern themselves? Or, more importantly, to what extent does changing the size, scope, and bias of a municipality fundamentally alter the distribution of power and resources within a locality?

CHAPTER 1

Size, Scope, and Bias: What Differentiates Local Electoral Politics?

ON APRIL 7, 2009, voters in the Illinois towns of Lyons, Carpentersville, Palatine, and Bensenville did something unusual—they did not reelect their governing mayors. Reporting on these results, the *Chicago Tribune* speculated on why these candidates lost, a surprising event considering that most of their fellow incumbents in nearby towns won. For each place, the *Tribune* had a seemingly unique explanation: in Lyons, the serving mayor inadvertently made a series of sexist and racist remarks on tape; in Carpentersville, the village president had a long history of fights with the city council; in Palatine, the incumbent faced a challenge from a former star player for the Chicago Bears; and in Bensenville, a concerted effort from Chicago's neighboring Daley political organization unseated the incumbent because of his opposition to an airport expansion project.[1] But while these explanations sound plausible, there is no way of differentiating their factual basis from mere speculation. We have no idea if mayors are more likely to be unseated when they face former football stars or if making racist remarks is fatal to holding office, because we have no systematic explanations about how people vote in small-scale elections.

Why do we know so little about local elections? Part of the problem lies with our understanding of elections in general. Most political observers view elections the way Gertrude Stein saw roses—as categorically similar phenomena.[2] In other words, voters

---

[1] *Chicago Tribune*, April 7, 2009: http://newsblogs.chicagotribune.com/clout_st/2009/04/election-results-arlington-heights-aurora-bensenville-carpentersville-deerfield-des-plaines-elmhurst.html.

[2] Stein's famous quip "a rose is a rose is a rose" could be translated as "an election is an election is an election."

use the same mental calculus regardless of whether they are voting for mayor, city clerk, dogcatcher, or president.[3] But if this were the case, then not only would local elections hinge on the partisanship, economic performance, and candidate charisma that are so decisive in presidential elections, they also would be decided by the same factors and in the same way time and time again.

Yet, as the foregoing examples illustrate, this is clearly not the case. Elections are not all the same, and simple common sense would tell us that voting for president is much different than voting for a mayor, city clerk, or dogcatcher. In fact, unlike their national counterparts, local elections are usually nonpartisan, get little media attention, and seem to provide voters with little public information to differentiate candidates. Similarly, most local elections are often free of direct racial or ethnic appeals or the preoccupation with crime or unemployment that dominate the political agendas of most large cities. This is not to suggest that partisanship, issues, race, or any of the factors common in larger-scale elections will never be important in local contests. Sometimes they will and sometimes they won't. But currently, we have no way of knowing when these factors matter and when they do not.

This, however, leads to an even bigger challenge to understanding local elections: how do we also differentiate among the tens of thousands of local governments in the United States? For not only are elections for mayor in places like Clarkston, Georgia, and Steubenville, Ohio, different than elections for president, they are different from each other as well. And just as we don't know how, exactly, local elections are different from presidential ones, we also lack a mechanism for understanding how or why a local election in one place is likely to be different from that in another. And without such a framework, we ultimately have no way of distinguishing between the systematic forces that shape local politics from idiosyncratic events and parochial circumstance. In short, if we want to understand the dynamics of local democracy, we need to identify what separates the electoral politics of a municipality

---

[3] The paradigmatic examples of this are spatial models of voting that assume voters evaluate candidates relative to their "distance" on some ideological or other continuum.

from that of a nation, state, county, special district, or any other form of democracy.

This chapter outlines a relatively simple way of doing this. Across the universe of democracies, three characteristics are the most powerful and widely applicable predictors of their electoral politics: size, scope, and bias. Once we know a democracy's population (*size*), the magnitude of its constitutive powers (*scope*), and how uniformly it distributes its resources (*bias*), we can predict a great deal about who votes, who runs for office, and whether factors like incumbency, parties, ideology, issues, interest groups, and candidate charisma shape vote choices. In other words, we can best predict how people will vote in a particular election if we first understand what is distinctive about that democracy's politics and, if we know its size, scope, and bias, we can predict what those electoral politics are like. To better understand this, let us separately examine the political dynamics of size, scope, and bias in more detail.

Size: the Power of Numbers

In 2010 voters in California and Vermont both elected governors, and while the formal powers of the two state offices are roughly similar, the contrast between the two elections could not have been greater. In California, Jerry Brown and Meg Whitman collectively spent over $200 million dollars on their campaigns, largely on television ads targeting key voters. Yet comparatively few Californians got to actually meet either candidate, let alone ask them any questions or express their views. For most Californians, Brown and Whitman were simply television personalities. In Vermont, Peter Shulman and Brian Dubie collectively spent under $2 million and ran far fewer television ads. Instead, they campaigned in the "old-fashioned" manner of going to town meetings, posting yard signs and billboards, meeting with prominent groups, holding public events, and even standing on street corners waving at cars passing by. Vermonters had many opportunities to personally interact with both candidates and make their assessments from first-hand experience.

The contrasting examples of California and Vermont highlight a long-standing concern among political philosophers: how big should a democracy be? Historically, philosophers have favored smaller population sizes. For example, Plato calculated that a republic should have no more than 5,000 citizens; Montesquieu thought democracies should not exceed 20,000 citizens. These calculations stemmed from normative concerns about the mechanisms of popular rule. Plato and Montesquieu believed that in order for citizens to have an effective and meaningful voice in public affairs, they needed to have direct access to their elected representatives and the governing processes. Democracies consisting of millions or tens of millions of people were unfathomable to premodern philosophers because the aggregation and coordination of so many different citizens' preferences seemed impossible, particularly in an era before mass literacy and popular media. And even while contemporary technology allows for easier communication between citizens and their representatives, the concerns of the classic philosophers about democratic accountability and citizen involvement continue to hold today. In an era of media-packaged, television-centered campaigns, many commentators justifiably fear that politicians lose accountability to the concerns of the mass public (Dahl and Tufte 1973).

In reality, an increased population size is both a blessing and a curse for any democracy. On the positive side, larger size allows for democracies to accomplish grander projects and achieve greater economies of scale in their governing operations (Alessina and Spoalare 2003). Few villages, for example, can construct the zoos, parks, civic centers, airports, and other amenities that are common in most large cities, and most towns actually provide fewer services directly than do larger cities. Data from the 2002 Census of Governments indicate that places with populations of less than 5,000 provide fewer than five of twenty basic services on average compared to nearly nine services offered in places over 100,000 in population.[4] These size effects work at nearly every level of gov-

---

[4] These possible services include airports, ambulance, cemeteries, jails, election offices, fire stations, gas, health bureaus, hospitals, housing, police, library, nursing homes, parks, mass transit, sewage, waste, street repair, and water.

ernment: Smaller towns are less likely to provide public housing, build hospitals, or have energy or waste treatment facilities than larger ones; Vermont could never sustain California's world-class public university system and finds it proportionately more costly to run many public services; small countries do not have space programs, build super-colliders, or sustain large militaries. Simply by virtue of its size, a larger democracy is going to be more powerful, and usually more efficient, than a smaller one.[5]

On the negative side, governmental accountability and access is lower in a large democracy than a small one. Partly, this is a simple problem of sheer logistics. A democracy's ability to consider the viewpoints, opinions, and perspectives of all its citizens diminishes exponentially with every new member it adds. These coordination challenges are especially difficult with governing decisions where citizens are likely to have strong opinions and varying degrees of information. No large city, for example, could reasonably govern itself according to the practices of a New England town meeting—there simply wouldn't be enough time for everyone to speak nor even a venue large enough to accommodate all citizens. As democracies become larger they must delegate more deliberative processes to experts, who, by necessity, will become increasingly distant from all citizens. In larger democracies, preferences must be expressed more through ratification than deliberation.

More importantly, larger democracies face bigger challenges to governing from their greater social heterogeneity. Large nations like the United States, India, Indonesia, and Brazil tend to have a higher amount of ethnic, regional, and class diversity, while smaller democracies like Denmark, Costa Rica, and Greece tend to be more homogeneous.[6] Data from the World Values survey indicate that countries under a million in size have, on average, a Social Diversity Index Score (Okediji 2005) of .68 on a 0 to 1 scale; this compares to an average score of .83 for countries over 25

---

[5] This also holds true for nongovernmental democratic organizations as well. Larger churches can reach more people and conduct more programs, larger nonprofits can take on more ambitious projects, and so on.

[6] Of course, this is not a hard and fast rule: Japan is very large yet relatively homogenous; Switzerland and Belgium are much smaller and yet more diverse.

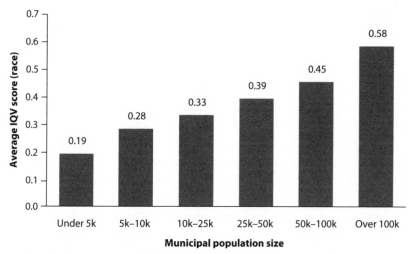

Figure 1.1. Average Score of Racial Diversity (IQV) by municipal population size. *Source*: 2000 U.S. Census (ncases = 23,760).

million in size. This trend also holds for American local govern-ments, as illustrated in figure 1.1. Looking at just one possible measure of diversity, race, we see that American municipalities consistently grow more racially heterogeneous as they get larger. Places under 5,000 in size have an average Index of Qualitative Variation (IQV) score, a measure of racial homogeneity, of only .19; places over 100,000 have an average score of .58.[7] The same trend occurs with nearly every other social category, including in-come, age, religion, and lifestyle choice—larger American cities tend to be more socially diverse than small ones.

For all these reasons, even as democracies grow larger and more capable, the connections between citizens and politicians grow more remote, mediated, and formally structured. Such effects also

---

[7] The index of qualitative variation measures the distribution of the population across discrete categories such as the ratio of the amount of observed variation to the amount of variation that could actually exist. The scores range from 0 (no variation) to 1 (maximum variation). The computational formula for the IQV is IQV = $k(N^2 - \Sigma (f^2)) / N^2 (k - 1)$, where k = number of categories (in this case five racial categories of white, black, Latino, Asian, and other), N = sum of cases and $\Sigma(f^2)$ = the sum of the squared frequencies.

have electoral repercussions. Smaller democracies may afford opportunities for deliberation, interpersonal persuasion, and immediate accountability, but are also usually limited in the range of decisions they need to adjudicate. A New England town meeting may provide an opportunity for all residents to express their opinions and to deliberate town decisions, but these decisions are usually going to be limited to a rather narrow range of issues.[8]

In larger democracies, the greater magnitude of political decisions, the increasing distance among citizens, and the greater diversity in their preferences mean that political processes will become more rationalized, organized, and systematic. With their larger projects and more heterogeneous populations, larger democracies will typically sprout more formally organized political groups. For instance, when a town grows big enough to support an airport, a new set of political constituencies is created among the landowners who wish to sell their properties to the airport authority, the local businesses who seek to profit from increased commerce, and the residents who may be adversely affected by noise and safety considerations. These political constituencies may manifest themselves as a political party or formal interest group such as an industry or environmental organization. Such organizations are less likely to emerge in smaller democracies not only because there are fewer issues of magnitude that could divide a more homogeneous membership base, but because aggregating member preferences is so much easier. A political party or formal interest group is simply unnecessary when a single candidate can directly contact all the voters and ask for their support. But when a political leader wants to rally thousands or millions of supporters, direct contact is simply unfeasible, and so an organization that mobilizes and coordinates political activists becomes a necessity.

The gubernatorial campaigns in Vermont and California provide typical examples of these tendencies. Candidates in Vermont

[8]A classic example of this might be a faculty meeting of a typical university department. Decisions on whom to hire or promote usually are voted on after every faculty member has had a chance to air his or her opinion. The nature of the discussions and debates can often be quite heated and influenced by personality more than issues. The stakes of such decisions, however, are likely to be relatively minor, which, if political scientist Wallace Sayre's "law" is correct, only makes the politicking all that much more fierce.

spend most of their campaign funds on staffing, billboards, yard signs, and bumper stickers, and very little on television advertising. This is partly because Vermont is a small media market (and thus cheaper to advertise in) but also because the small size of the state allows for politics to have a more retail flavor. Voters in Vermont expect to meet their politicians in person, and a large percentage of Vermonters actually will have met the candidates. In California, the idea of a candidate trying to personally meet even a small fraction of her state's 37 million residents is ludicrous. Political campaigns in California thus mean lots of media consultants, television advertisements, mass mailings, and well-calculated voter mobilization drives. Because so few of California's voters have any direct contact with their candidates, party labels also become much more important as guides for orienting their voting behavior.

A democracy's size not only influences the logic of political organization, but also who votes, who runs for office, and the levels of voter information about local campaigns. Past research has shown that residents of larger cities tend to vote less than residents of smaller places partly because they are less interested in local affairs or less familiar with local leaders (Oliver 2001). Similarly, we would also expect that candidates in larger places will be more ambitious in their political aspirations and professional in their political skills, simply because the investment of time, effort, and resources in running for office in a larger place is so much greater. And, as a democracy becomes larger and candidates rely more on mass media or reaching voters through particular groups, voter knowledge about candidates and campaigns may change. In smaller places, voters are more likely to be personally familiar with their office seekers; in larger places, they are less likely to know candidates, particularly if the contestants are not incumbents.

The likely impact of population size on municipal electoral politics is summarized in table 1.1. For simplicity's sake, municipalities are arbitrarily categorized by four levels of population size. The estimates in the table also derive from the assumption that a certain portion of a town (roughly 25 percent) is ineligible to vote because its inhabitants are too young, are not citizens, or do not meet other requirements. If we also assume a 25 percent turnout rate, this means the number of votes that a winning candidate ac-

TABLE 1.1
Hypothetical Changes in Electoral Politics by Town Size

Town Size	Typical Number of Votes Needed to Win	Type of Electoral Politics
Under 10,000	Up to 1,000	Mostly personal connections
10,000–50,000	1,000–5,000	Personal connections, group appeals
50,000–100,000	5,000–10,000	Group appeals, mass advertising
Over 100,000	Over 10,000	Mass advertising, group appeals

tually needs in order to attain local office can be quite small. For example, in a town of 4,000, only 3,000 residents may actually be eligible to vote. If only 25 percent of these turn out for a local election, a candidate needs only to secure just over half of the 750 votes (i.e., 376 votes) to win. With such a small number of votes required, the typical candidate can probably win election largely through personal contacts. Although most candidates would also seek to bolster their candidacy through yard signs, stickers, fliers, buttons, and the like, much of their support will come through more personal connections.

As municipalities become larger (say over 10,000 in population), the number of votes needed to win elections also grows and mandates a change in campaign strategy, because candidates will need to find conduits to larger numbers of voters. These could be appeals to particular groups, such as civic associations, local clubs, churches, or sports leagues. Although personal connections will still be important for places under 50,000 in population, many candidates will have to turn to organizations to more efficiently reach and mobilize voters. Once a town grows over 50,000 in size, candidates will mobilize voters primarily through mass advertising such as billboards, signs, mailings, and telephone banks. As a result, voters will base their decisions less on personal knowledge of candidates and more on either specific issues or heuristics such as partisanship, name recognition, or positions on key issues. Of course, even in the largest town, politicians will probably still try to personally meet as many voters as possible, but the firsthand acquaintanceships that candidates have with most of their supporters is a resource available only to the small-town official.

When a candidate's campaign strategy hinges on mobilizing certain groups, the question arises as to which groups he or she should be contacting. This depends on the political climate of the community. Obviously, the smart politician will seek to cultivate those constituents who are most likely to vote for him or her, creating two important parts to this calculation: which constituents are most likely to vote and which of these are most likely to be supportive. How a candidate decides these factors will depend largely on the dimensions of scope and bias, which will be detailed later on. Thus while population size has implications for the kinds of campaign strategies that are necessary to win, it will not be able to provide much information about specific campaign tactics, particularly in the absence of information about the other two dimensions.

Nevertheless, when focusing just on population size and electoral politics, we can deduce the following hypotheses:

- As democracies grow in size, they typically face a wider range of political issues, become more socially heterogeneous, and have fewer personal interconnections among their citizens.
- Consequently, in electoral campaigns in larger democracies there will be fewer personal contacts between voters and candidates, and the elections will center more around advertising, interest group mobilization, and mass media.
- Elections in larger democracies will be more professionalized and fiercely contested because of the greater stakes involved and the types of candidates who are motivated to run.
- The wider array of issues and the more heterogeneous constituencies that abound in larger democracies create incentives for the formation of political organizations such as parties and interest groups, which will also serve as conduits to voters.
- In smaller democracies, voters will have more personal contact with candidates, be more interested and knowledgeable about local politics, and base their voting decisions on parochial issues, whereas in larger democracies, voters are more likely to utilize heuristics to make decisions, such as party labels, group endorsements, or candidate name recognition.

Scope: Existential Versus Managerial Democracy

Despite being on nearly opposite sides of the planet, the country of San Marino and the suburb of San Dimas share a lot in common. They have roughly the same population size; they both enjoy Mediterranean climates (one on the Italian peninsula, the other in California), low crime rates, and a high standard of living; and, they are both democracies that elect governing councils and executives. Yet, despite all of these similarities, their electoral politics could not be more different. The Most Serene Republic of San Marino (its formal name) has numerous political parties, including two communist ones, that fiercely contest its elections. Political campaigns are intense and voters are bombarded with existential appeals about deep and divisive visions over the fundamental nature of their tiny nation. Its highly ideological parties are continually shifting in a constellation of unstable alliances in order to reach governing majorities. San Dimas, by contrast, has nonpartisan elections, stable governing coalitions, and a comparatively tranquil political atmosphere. In the 2009 election, the incumbents all got over 75 percent of the vote. Campaigns in San Dimas rarely touch on any ideological divisions, and the idea of even one communist, socialist, fascist, or fundamentalist party is farfetched at best. So why, given their same size, economic affluence, and other similarities, do the electoral politics in San Marino and San Dimas differ so dramatically?

The most obvious answer is the *scope* of the offices being contested. Scope refers to a democracy's capacity for action, the extent to which it can exercise autonomous discretion over the people, businesses, and other institutions in the geographic area it governs. In lay terms, scope refers to how much power a democracy wields. A democracy's scope can be determined by any number of factors, ranging from its wealth to the willingness of its citizens to acquiesce to governmental decisions. While all of these influences are important, for the purposes of this book, I will focus primarily on two institutional determinants of scope. The first is the powers formally invested in the democracy through its charter, constitution, or other founding documents; in other words, the explicitly stated rules outlining the breadth and limitations of its authority. The second is the extent to which a democracy's governing arrangements enable or inhibit decisive action on the part of its leaders. A democracy may have unlimited powers but demand so much power sharing and consensus among its elected officials that government is effectively restricted in its ability to pursue policy agendas. In sum, scope consists of both the formal rules that outline its powers and the institutional arrangements that determine how governing decisions get made.

To better illustrate the concept of scope, let us return to the examples just mentioned. Despite its small size, San Marino is relatively high in scope because it is a sovereign nation and national government is basically unlimited government. Nation-states can do whatever they want within their borders because they exercise *ultimate sovereignty*. They determine who is a citizen and what rights that citizen holds; they delimit a person's freedoms and very identity; they claim the supreme monopoly on the legitimate use of force; they control currency and regulate trade across borders; they establish property rights and taxes; they can specify what language its citizens speak, what information they have access to, and their very social organization. Thus San Marino, for example, could raise an army, exclude any visitors, socialize all private property, ban marriage, and require all of its residents to speak Swahili if it so desired.

The city of San Dimas, on the other hand, is a democracy narrow in scope because it is a local government, and local government is, by definition, limited government. San Dimas is not simply constrained by its size (after all, San Marino is just as small), but also by the statutory limits placed on it by the superior state and federal governments. It is an underappreciated fact that municipal governments are formally institutional subunits of their respective states. They exist largely at the discretion of their larger state governments and most have highly constrained powers. For example, until the imposition of "home rule," most municipalities could not pass ordinances, create departments, or even hire employees without state approval. Even today, a huge and complicated municipal government like New York City still has to get state approval if it wants to initiate many types of policies. For example, New York State recently rejected a proposal by the city to impose a traffic congestion zone in midtown Manhattan. State governments could choose, at any time, to dissolve a particular municipality or subsume its responsibilities under some other structure of governance.

As a result, most municipalities have little latitude in the range of activities they can pursue. They cannot, as political scientist Paul Peterson reminds us, issue currency, restrict the movement of capital or populations, or create an army.[9] Instead, municipalities are bound mostly to issues of land-usage (such as zoning ordinances and utility provision) or local quality of life (such as ordinances on noise or public behavior). This is not to imply that such issues are less important. In fact, they may have a tremendous impact on the daily lives of ordinary citizens. Local ordinances can even be quite draconian in their capacity of shaping citizen behavior. Nevertheless, it is a simple fact that municipalities are limited in terms of what *types* of issues they can pursue.[10]

The limited scope of local governments can be well illustrated by examining the range of services that they actually offer. Table 1.2 lists the percent of municipalities under 100,000 in population that provide nineteen possible government services commonly offered by municipal governments, according to the 2002 U.S. Census of Governments. Roughly half of all local governments directly provide six services: street repair, parks, water, sewage, police, and fire protection. Roughly 20 percent provide libraries and cemeteries, less than 15 percent provide solid waste removal, ambulance services, and public housing, less than 10 percent provide elec-

---

[9] For an excellent discussion of this, see Peterson 1981.

[10] The same also holds true for most other democratic organizations. Civic associations, churches, unions, corporate boards, nonprofits, and virtually any other type of nongovernmental democratic organization almost always have a charter or specific bylaws that delimit their particular powers. These not only define the prerogatives of executives but also the general mission of the organization. Garden clubs, teachers' unions, or Elks Lodges cannot simply decide to raise armies, pass laws that would affect nonmembers, or even decide to construct roads or highways. Although some organizations do expand their scope or change their missions over time (the March of Dimes is a classic example), most subnational democratic organizations are constitutionally bound to focus on a specific set of tasks.

TABLE 1.2
Percent of Municipalities under 100,000 in Population Providing
Direct Provision of the Nineteen Most Commonly Offered Local
Government Services

Street Repair	55%
Parks	53%
Water	52%
Sewage	51%
Police	48%
Fire	45%
Library	21%
Cemeteries	20%
Solid Waste	15%
Ambulance	13%
Public Housing	12%
Electric Utility	7%
Airport	6%
Gas Utility	4%
Jail	4%
Public Health	2%
Mass Transit	2%
Nursing Homes	1%
Hospital	.5%

Source: 2002 U.S. Census of Governments; ncases = 17,893.

tricity or airports, and less than 5 percent provide the remaining
services such as jails, mass transit, nursing homes, and hospitals.

This list is notable in several respects. First, many local services
are not provided directly by municipalities but, instead, are offered
by counties or special district governments. In fact, the trend over
the past three decades has been for local services to be increasingly
provided by special district governments (Berry 2009), a move that
furthers the political fragmentation, and possibly limits the democratic accountability, of local governments. Indeed, some may
argue that the efforts of local governments to intentionally limit
government services in order to sustain low tax rates yet enjoy

the autonomy of local incorporation (i.e., a "Lakewood" plan) was itself a decidedly political act (Miller 1981). This issue will be taken up further in chapter 6. Second, the services that local governments most often provide, while having a big impact on their communities, are not ones that facilitate a great deal of redistribution or, with the exception of police protection, the exertion of much coercive control over a population. Rather, these are mostly services surrounding the provision and maintenance of basic infrastructure needs: water, sewage, power, and transportation. It is as much for the minor types of services it provides as for the range of services that it statutorily can provide, that local government is limited government.

Of course, local governments are not toothless. They do pass ordinances and laws that forbid or regulate a large range of individual and commercial activities. Typically these include issues around zoning, construction, and commercial activity, but local governments also influence individual behaviors such as gambling, animals care, bicycle riding, garbage disposal, obscenity, noise, parties and parades, begging and loitering, smoking, clothing and public nudity, and one's general demeanor in public places. Often times, such regulations can be quite extensive or particularistic: in Dennison, Texas, it is illegal for a woman to adjust her stockings in public; in Tremonton, Utah, women can be arrested for having sex in an ambulance (although men are not subject to the law); in Half Moon Bay, California, it is a misdemeanor to wear a sweatshirt inside out (Pelton 1990). It is in the regulation of their residents' ordinary behaviors that local governments often exercise their greatest power. Nevertheless, because such regulations fall under the domain of state and federal law (and are often overturned because of their conflicts with such laws), local governments still do not have the same level of scope as their super-ordinate institutions. Local governments may forbid stocking adjustment, ambulatory fornication, and wearing clothes inside out, but such laws can (and often are) overturned by state or national governments, which further constrains the scope of municipalities.

Beyond its constitutive powers, a democracy's scope is also determined by the extent to which its powers are concentrated or distributed among its elected officials. Democracies that force executive and legislative branches to share powers have less scope than those whose powers are concentrated in a unified branch, simply because any government action requires a greater consensus among a larger group of political interests (Lipjhart 1999). For all its size and economic clout, a presidential democracy like the United States has less scope than a parliamentary democracy like Great Britain because, in the latter, both executive and legislative branches are controlled by the same party whereas in the former, the executive and legislative branches are elected separately yet must share powers. The difficulty that President Barack Obama experienced in passing health care legislation in 2010 even as his party controlled both houses of Congress is testament to the very limitations that were intentionally placed on the American government by the framers of its constitution. Such hindrances would have been unimaginable to Gordon Brown, the former prime minister of Great Britain, because his executive leadership is a byproduct of his party's absolute control of parliament.[11]

The same principle holds for local governments as well. Municipalities with "strong mayor" governments (i.e., those where the mayor has power to appoint department heads and draft budgets) have a lot more scope than "weak mayor" or "council-manager" governments, where appointments and decisions depend on achieving majority or super-majorities in governing councils. In the United States, it has been long recognized that when decisions are made by a single individual mayor or town executive, then that office will have more power, both for good and ill (Hamilton, Madison, and Jay [1789] 1961). Indeed, this was precisely the logic of the "reform" movement that animated the movement away from mayoral governments and partisan elections during the Progressive Era (Teaford 1979).

Both the constitutive and power-sharing aspects of a democracy's scope have a major impact on its electoral politics. This is foremost evident in the ideological tone of the race. Because of their greater scope, elections for national offices are existential contests—people vote not merely to indicate their policy prefer-

---

[11]David Cameron, Brown's successor as prime minister, had less scope because his parliamentary majority came from a coalition between his conservative party and a third party.

ences, but also to express their ideology, ethnic or religious affiliations, or other markers of self-conception. This is one reason why
a tiny country like San Marino has so many ideological political
parties: its elections are mechanisms of self-identification not just
of governance. Patriotism, moral rectitude, and ethnic identity are
salient in national elections, not because they displace issues of
policy but because national elections are existentially relevant. In
such places, the vote becomes a mechanism for expressing one's
own vision of a society, a vision that is often in zero-sum competition with other visions.

Elections in limited-scope democracies, by contrast, are more
managerial than existential. Such elections are rarely contests over
broader visions about how society in general should be organized
and governed. Although ideological or group-related issues may
sometimes arise in local races, the limited nature of most small-
scale offices tends to preclude existential politics, because the types
of services provided local governments do not lend themselves to
sharp ideological distinctions. Services like street repair, sewage,
or fire protection are difficult to administer in a "conservative" or
"liberal" manner.

Furthermore, those areas where local governments can exercise
a lot of scope (i.e., municipal ordinances regarding public behavior
and private property) may be the subject of ideological contestation, but these conflicts are likely to be parochial and temporal in
nature. Most municipal ordinances deal with quality of life issues
and are implemented to reduce conflict among neighbors. Because
they typically do not deal with the collection or distribution of
public resources, these regulations usually do not generate long-
standing political constituencies. Consider the example of Sara-
sota, Florida, which passed a law prohibiting people from singing
in public while wearing a bathing suit. Such a peculiar regulation may be designed to promote "public decency," but it is hard
to imagine a chronic political battle continually fought between
bikini-clad choristers and the Sarasotans they offend. Perhaps
these ordinances will prompt an occasional political campaign or
movement, but where and how such ordinances arise and such
political activities emerge is nearly impossible to predict.

Ideological politics in American municipalities are further limited by fiscal restraints. After meeting statutory mandates from their state governments about what services they must provide, there is often little discretionary money available for pursuing larger social projects. State governments demand that, as a necessary requirement for municipal incorporation, towns and cities make provisions for police, fire, water, sewage, and general public safety, and these services often make up the lion's share of the municipal budget. Consequently, even the most entrepreneurial local politician will be unable to promise the type of policy agenda common on the national stage. Local politicians can't declare war or change interest rates, and few would be able to enact universal health care or social insurance for residents. If the municipality shares overlapping jurisdictions with other special district governments, then the elected official may have even fewer options. If a town also has an independent school district, transit district, water reclamation district, and park district, then many of the most salient issues facing municipalities (education, transportation, and open space) simply may be irrelevant to local politics.

The managerial character of most local governments is exacerbated by the mobility of their residents. If the citizens of a nation-state are unhappy with the leaders, they can emigrate, but such a costly move means renouncing their citizenship and fundamentally changing their identity. Given the high expenditures of such an "exit" option, citizens are more likely to contest national politics more vigorously (Hirschman 1970). But if residents of a town are unhappy with the politics or policies of their community, moving is a much less onerous burden. Indeed, the power of mobility has inspired a whole school of thought about local governance. According to "public choice" theorists, political fragmentation and competition promote individual self-sorting relative to public services and taxes (Tiebout 1956). Parents will seek suburbs with good schools, elderly residents will seek suburbs with lower property taxes, etc. In short, people will influence local policy not by voting at the ballot box, but by "voting with their feet." A high level of self-sorting will then produce smaller communities in a metropolitan area that are more internally homogeneous but externally differentiated. Some places will have better schools, others lower taxes, and others more opportunities for economic development. This homogenization will further diminish ideological conflict and create greater consensus about what the character of the community and the mission of local government should be.

Another major difference between managerial and existential democracy is in the criteria that voters use to evaluate their candidates. Voters in any election face the dilemma of guaranteeing how their candidates will behave once in office. Will they keep their promises? Will they be corrupt or good administrators? Will they make wise decisions or foolish ones? To answer these questions, voters may rely on a variety of information sources. Some of these are "prospective" heuristics, information shortcuts about how a candidate is likely to behave once in office. Such prospective cues may be a party label or the candidates' professed issue positions, but they could also include other pieces of information such as a candidate's biography. The other information sources will come from the performance of incumbents while in office, what political scientists often refer to as "retrospective" evaluations. These retrospective cues can be based on considerations like the state of the economy, personal scandals, or institutional malfeasance.

Although voters in both high- and low-scope democracies will employ prospective and retrospective evaluations, the criteria they will use to make these evaluations will differ sharply. In high-scope democracies with existential elections, both prospective and retrospective evaluations will hinge primarily on party loyalties and ideological divisions. Not only will voters base their future expectations on what party a candidate is from, they will also evaluate the past performance of incumbents based on partisan considerations as well. For example, in U.S. presidential elections, partisans of an incumbent president are far more likely to offer positive evaluations regarding the state of the economy or the functioning of government than nonpartisans (Bartels 1996).

In low-scope or managerial democracies, prospective and retrospective evaluations will be less colored by ideology or party, and more by incumbents' performance relative to the parameters of the institution. Once a locality has adopted a particular range of services and level of taxation, its leaders will be judged more on how well they administer these tasks as an institution or on their stances on community-specific issues rather than on what type of political vision they have for society at large. In other words, candidates will be judged less on whether they are liberals or conservatives, Democrats or Republicans, but on the quality of services they provide relative to the amount of taxes being levied. Much like a corporate board evaluating a business' management team, voters in managerial elections will evaluate local leaders on how good a job they are doing relative to the specific mandates of their institutions and the particular histories of their communities (Lewis and Neiman 2009). For example, voters in a residential suburb will look at property values, crime rates, or school test scores (Berry and Howell 2007); voters in a historic suburb may consider development issues and preservation (Fischel 2001); voters in commercial suburb may look at traffic or property taxes—and so forth.

In general, most citizens will probably use common-sense heuristics to evaluate local performance: Are taxes going up? Are services being cut or declining in quality? Are potholes being filled or is trash being picked up? As long as basic operations run smoothly and incumbents avoid being on the wrong side of a very visible issue or caught in a scandal, voters in most localities will probably not need to seek any more information and incumbents should have an easy time getting elected. After all, most voters should be averse to fixing any institution that is not already broken.

The managerial character of low-scope democracies also puts differing types of political pressure on their politicians. The challenge for all elected officials is to communicate their successes, rally their supporters, and avoid political pitfalls. The ability to do this depends largely on the authority that their office holds, the extent they will face conflicting political demands, and their success in sustaining networks of political support. Research on comparative retrospective voting finds that incumbents in national elections who have more clearly defined responsibilities and greater concentrated powers are more likely to be punished for economic downturns than incumbents who share powers (Powell and Whitten 1993). The same process is likely to occur at the local level. Municipal officials who are responsible for a wider range of services or confront a broader range of issues are more likely to incur the displeasure of divided constituencies; simply by having to make more decisions, they are likely to displease more people. A mayor or city council that has to close schools or authorize a new roadway is bound to alienate at least some group of citizens. At the same time, their greater power also gives them more opportunities to cultivate specific political constituencies. A "strong" mayor may take greater blame for a town's problems, but he or she also has much greater leverage in dispensing political patronage and rewarding political supporters. If a town mayor has no control over schools, cedes development authority to a park district or water district, and is absolved from funding a fire department (often the most expensive budget item for a small municipality), there will be fewer contentious items that would divide the citizenry but fewer resources to build networks of support.

In sum, the relative paucity of governmental responsibilities and the particular nature of their powers mean that local elections primarily will be determined by incumbent performance relative to a preexisting tax/service equilibrium (Berry 2009). Citizens are likely to become accustomed to a certain status quo regarding the types of services they expect and the taxes they pay. As long as incumbents perform their custodial responsibilities adequately and avoid major changes, they are likely to be reelected.

When local elections deviate from this pattern, it will usually occur for two reasons. First, the democracy is so socially heterogeneous that chronic political divisions cause ongoing conflict. For example, a community that holds a lot of valuable but undeveloped land will probably face greater political conflict between business interests who want to maximize property values and home-owners who want to conserve the "green space" in their community. Here, elections will move away from pure referenda on incumbency and be more oriented toward the ongoing political divisions, as long as they last. In the case of the community with the land issues, one would expect "pro-development" candidates running against "anti-development" ones, until the issue of the land development gets resolved. However, since most American localities are fairly homogenous and lack many of the clearly identifiable political cleavages that exist in larger democracies (Oliver 2001), such chronic political fights will be less common.

Second, incumbents are likely to be unseated when random events or exogenous shocks upset the standard operating procedure. In managerial democracies, political divisions may arise over more idiosyncratic or particular events, such as a scandal, an inopportune political comment, or personal indiscretion. This makes local elections somewhat less predictable. For not only are political divisions in managerial democracies less common, they also have more of a random quality to them. No one knows if an off-handed comment could be interpreted in a wrong way or if some citizen will become so indignant over a minor municipal decision that he or she decides to run for office.

Considering the differences in scope across all democracies, we can thus deduce the following hypotheses about their electoral politics:

- The greatest differences in the electoral politics between national and local democracies are due to the scope of the offices being contested.
- Elections in broad-scope democracies, such as nation-states, are likely to be existential, and thus more ideological in character and more focused on the deep questions of the role of the state and society.
- Elections in limited-scope democracies, such as municipalities, are more managerial in character and deal more with the custodial duties of the office.
- In managerial democracies, voter decisions will usually be a referendum on incumbent custodial performance, although the criteria by which incumbent performance is judged may vary according to other factors in the organization, such as its size or bias.
- The electoral politics of managerial democracies will vary according to how much power is concentrated in the executive office; in places with "strong" executives, greater incentives exist for the formation of strong political parties or other interest groups.

- Incumbents in managerial democracies should do better the fewer their official responsibilities and the less social or economic conflict within their jurisdiction, particularly if they also have more discretionary power.
- The overall lack of divisive political conflicts in most managerial democracies makes it very difficult to anticipate when salient political issue arise and when incumbents will be unseated.

Bias: To the Victor Go the Spoils

At first glance, it would be natural to assume that the electoral politics of Nassau County, New York, and Contra Costa County, California, would be very similar. Both are suburban counties in large metropolitan areas (the former of New York City, the latter of San Francisco) that lack a major, central city within their borders. They are very similar in population size, affluence, and racial composition. Both counties are responsible for similar types of public services such as roads, utilities, health care, and police protection. And, in terms of presidential elections, both areas are very similar in their voting patterns: they were both once Republican strongholds that have voted more Democratic over the past two decades.

Yet, despite these similarities, the electoral politics in Contra Costa and Nassau counties are quite different. Elections to Contra Costa's five-person county board are generally low-key events. Incumbents often run unopposed and a high degree of consensus occurs among the board members. There are few issues that galvanize its residents or make its elections subject to much scrutiny. Elections in Nassau County, on the other hand, are highly partisan and very contentious. Over the past sixty years, Nassau county has been itinerantly governed by a Republican political machine that in the late 1990s nearly bankrupted one of America's most affluent areas through uneven tax breaks, large amounts of political hiring, and overinflated government contracts and other services. Nassau officials were notorious for cutting property taxes for their supporters, awarding large contracts to political cronies, and putting friends and family members on staff with inflated salaries. Its elections were often referenda on such machine politics, and the longevity of the county Republican organization was testament to its skillful use of political resources to maintain itself in power.

These contrasting examples highlight the third important characteristic that differentiates democracies, their *bias*. By bias, I refer to the extent to which costs and benefits are unevenly distributed among a democracy's constituents. At one end of the bias spectrum are democracies whose services and tax burdens are equally distributed to all constituent members, what political scientist Douglas Arnold (1992) refers to as "general costs." Examples of such "universalistic" or "unbiased" democracies might be an independent fire district in which the residents' uniform taxes all go to support fire protection, which is indiscriminately applied, or a condominium board that charges all residents the same fee to hire contractors for waste management and cleaning for the entire building. At the other end of the spectrum are the "biased" democracies, which direct their resources to a small number of specified constituencies while still extracting revenues from a large swath of the citizenry. In his study of congressional policy making, Arnold (1992) refers to a similar phenomenon as "group costs." For democracies in general, this bias can be organized in very systematic ways, as with a political machine that utilizes patronage to secure votes; but bias can also be less systematic, as when a particular interest group is able to secure specific regulations, protections, or resources that come at the expense of the greater whole.

Most democracies inevitably exist somewhere in between these two extremes since the variety of policies they are responsible for vary in their costs and since the very nature of governance makes purely universalistic or purely biased administrations extremely difficult to sustain. Consider the example of the universalistic fire district. Although all residents of the fire district may pay taxes to the special district government, they cannot enjoy equal fire protection simply because those residents who live closer to fire stations are going to be served more quickly. Similarly, the fire district will need to hire workers, employ contractors, and purchase other goods and whoever receives these contracts, if they live in the district, will disproportionately benefit. On the other side, few democracies can be entirely biased because, by definition, they still rely on the support of their constituent members. As a democracy's resources get directed toward fewer members (i.e., it gets more biased), it is more likely to incur the wrath of the disadvantaged majority. Even political machines still need to perform basic government services lest they be thrown out of office (Fuchs 1992).

Because of these complexities, bias is also a much more difficult characteristic to specify than either size or scope. While a democracy's population size can be counted or its formal powers documented, the extent of its bias is less quantifiable and more subjectively determined. There are numerous reasons why this is the case:

- Nearly every governmental decision is likely to affect some citizens more than others: citizens who use libraries or parks more will benefit disproportionately from these services; homeowners living near a roadway may be affected adversely by the decision to widen the streets; and so on.

- Some citizens may have preferences for certain kinds of malapportioned resources, thus raising the question of whether governmental bias can really be considered as bias if all citizens favor it. For example, most national and state governments redistribute funds to the poor in accordance with the wishes of a majority of citizens. Wealthy people may support a welfare program they will never use because they draw comfort in knowing that their indigent neighbors are not destitute.

- Some redistributive programs may have greater spillover effects for an entire community, as when a local government provides tax breaks for businesses or property developments to bolster economic growth or provide community amenities.

- Some policies, like public education or even a water district, may seem biased because not all citizens receive direct benefits of the government but nevertheless such services are still *available* to them.

- Even seemingly nonbiased governmental programs can be administered in a biased fashion: police officers may patrol some neighborhoods more than others; fire stations are closer to some homes than others; the snow gets plowed on some streets before others; and so forth.

Given the inherently subjective nature of this dimension, how can we determine the amount of a democracy's bias? Although bias is a chronically slippery concept, there will be at least five factors that are indicative of the mal-apportionment of a democracy's costs and benefits. First are the types of policies that governments pursue. In most industrialized democracies, national governments engage in a large number of "transfer" payments to the poor and the elderly. For example, in the United States, this includes social security, Medicare, Medicaid, and food stamps. Many state governments and some counties also have similar programs that are often supplemental to federal redistribution policies. Few municipalities, however, engage in such direct redistributions. As noted earlier, the programs that most municipalities provide (fire and police protection, roads, sewers, and water provision) are generally universal types of programs, available to and utilized by most residents. This is partly a function of municipalities' limited scope and the high degree of political fragmentation found in most American political communities. Most localities cannot pursue massive redistribution efforts because of state laws that bar them from doing so and because of competitive pressures with nearby towns (Peterson 1981).

Second, although one cannot know if a democracy is allocating resources in a biased way unless one is familiar with its internal politics, evidence of bias may be seen in its spending patterns. And even though it is hard to compare spending patterns among national, state, and local governments because they pursue such different types of policies, one can compare nations, states, or localities with each other. Democracies that spend more per capita than comparable places may be doing so because of political pressures to sustain biased programs (Trounstine 2008). In other words, if one compares two equally poor democracies, the one that spends more per capita is a better candidate to have a biased allocation system.

Third, bias may also be evident in a democracy's electoral arrangements. At a national level, bias could be manifest in campaign finance rules or the way legislative districts are drawn: democracies that allow interest groups to dominate campaign contributions or partisans to gerrymander political districts are likely to have more biased policies—after all, why else would a business group or labor union spend large amounts of money on campaigns if they did not expect to reap political rewards? At the local level, other institutional structures may be in place to promote political patronage. These could include partisan or district elections, the concentration of hiring and contracting decisions in an elected executive, or scheduling elections for unusual times. In a notable example of this, political scientist Sarah Anzia finds that in school districts with off-cycle elections, teachers have higher average salaries, a fact she attributes to the disproportionate power of teachers' unions (Anzia 2011). Although "reform style" governments sometimes generate biased allocations (Bridges 1997; Trounstine 2008), institutional arrangements like a professional city manager or at-large electoral districts generally inhibit political patronage.

Fourth, a democracy's bias will also be a function of its affluence. Poor democracies are going to be inherently more biased simply because the costs and impact of any decision are felt more greatly among their citizens. As an example, consider the political importance of a garbage contract for a rich township like Princeton, New Jersey, compared to its impoverished neighbor Camden. With a median family income above $125,000 a year and an average home value of over $1 million, it is highly unlikely that many of Princeton's 16,000 residents work for garbage companies (although they may own one). When the township hires a garbage company, it is probably importing all its labor and services. On the other hand, a garbage contract for an impoverished place like Camden (with an unemployment rate well over 30 percent) means dozens of good jobs for its residents. When Camden hires a garbage company, its leaders will thus be under considerable political pressure to hire Camden residents and to employ a locally operated firm. Camden officials who decide the garbage contract will, in turn, probably expect continued support from the company and its workers. The garbage contract, simply by virtue of Camden's poverty, will be a major source of political contestation whereas in Princeton it is simply a contract to be filled.

Fifth, bias will also be a function of a democracy's ethnic or racial composition. Given the long history of ethnic and racial disenfranchisement in the United States and the continuing power of race as a marker of social identity, racial politics are likely to emerge whenever a racial or ethnic minority is of a sufficient size in a population. This could take the form of purely symbolic representation on locally elected bodies but more often result in demands for specific resources to be distributed along racial or ethnic lines. For example, in a town where a minority group numbers 30 percent of the population, members of that group may expect that a proportionate number of municipal jobs, contracts, or services will be directed specifically toward that group. Other empirical studies on this topic support this assumption. For instance, in their study of major U.S. cities, counties, and metropolitan areas, economist Alberto Alesina and colleagues (Alesina, Baqir, and Easterly 1999) find that spending on universalistic public goods, like libraries, roads, and sewers, is inversely related to a community's ethnic diversity. Comparative studies of clientalism and ethnic voting also find that the distribution of public resources becomes more skewed as ethnic diversity increases (Wantchekon 2003; Olken 2007). Even when politicians seek to redress historical patterns of racial discrimination, the simple differentiation of beneficiaries on the basis of ethnicity or race causes a bias to emerge.

Of course, by themselves, each of these factors is not determinative of bias—a democracy can be racially mixed, poor, and have partisan elections without concentrating its resources among a limited group of its citizens. But, as noted, measuring bias is a very difficult task, and if one is looking for indications of bias, factors like income level, race, electoral arrangements, types of policies pursued, and spending patterns are likely to be a good source. Given this, the electoral politics of a biased democracy should look much different than those of a universalistic one. Bias, after all, is endogenous to the political process. Any group that significantly benefits from a democracy's bias will have much stronger incentives to vote, run candidates, or support favorable candidates. Such patterns are clearly evident at every level of American democracy: senior citizens (a great beneficiary of government entitlements) are more likely to vote in American national politics, property developers are more likely to run for local offices, and family and neighbors of party machine workers more likely to support machine bosses (Campbell 2005; Erie 1988).

In a biased democracy, political groups and personal networks are more likely to cohere in order to sustain the misallocation of public resources. These could be formal, hierarchical organizations like a political machine or informal networks of influential business leaders or activists who band together in a "growth regime" (Logan and Molotch 1987). Either way, wherever particularized resources exist, there are incentives for political organization on behalf of the beneficiaries. Group-based electoral appeals are probably more likely to occur in biased democracies than universalistic ones. When politicians link particular benefits to specific groups, such as social insurance for the elderly or affirmative action programs for minorities, they are likely to try to mobilize and target these groups as a part of their campaigns. Conversely, if the beneficiary group is small and the bias is great, one might also see politicians in biased democracies run as "reformers" who seek to implement more universalistic programs.

As a result of this, political cleavages in a highly biased democracy should be more visible. For example, in big cities, candidates who dispense patronage through political machines or ethnic social networks make themselves clearly known and often run against reform candidates who want more universalistic policies (Wolfinger 1974). Similarly, in school district elections, candidates supported by teachers' unions are well organized and often run in opposition to candidates who oppose the union's agenda (Anzia 2011). In places with low bias, by contrast, the political fault lines are much harder to identify. If all citizens are receiving equivalent levels of service, then it is unclear what political factors are going to divide them over the long haul. In other words, it is unlikely that people in a town are going to express long-standing division over an issue like fire protection, because they all get roughly the same level of public service. This also means that the electoral politics of a low-biased democracy are hard to specify and its electoral outcomes will be somewhat harder to predict. As with democracies low in scope, in democracies low in bias, incumbents should generally do well as long as they perform with a reasonable level of competence. However, the absence of enduring political cleavages also makes it difficult to predict when a decisive political event might occur. For incumbents in low-biased democracies, political challenges may arise from seemingly out of the blue or for the most petty of reasons.

Given these considerations, we can therefore deduce some hypotheses about the impact of bias in democratic elections:

- Bias will be a function of a democracy's electoral procedures, institutions, its social and political composition, and its affluence.
- The more biased a democracy is, the more its electoral politics will be contested by specific interest groups and structured around patronage networks.
- The greater the amount of bias (i.e., the fewer the number of beneficiaries and the larger their rewards), the more likely politicians will emerge who make "universalistic" appeals to contest established political interests.
- The dynamics of elections (who votes, who runs, and the nature of campaigns and vote choice) will be more predictable in biased democracies because their political divisions are more enduring and clearly identifiable.
- In less biased democracies, as with democracies low in scope, incumbents should do well, but decisive political issues are going to be hard to predict.

THE RELATIONSHIPS AMONG SIZE, SCOPE, AND BIAS

While the characteristics of size, scope, and bias each have a distinct effect on a democracy's electoral politics, they are not necessarily independent of each other; in fact, they are highly correlated. Larger democracies, simply by being bigger, also are going to have more scope than smaller ones. For example, nation-states are all high in scope because of their ultimate sovereignty, but some nations have even greater scope than others because of their larger populations and greater economies. A small country like Jamaica cannot develop a space program, build a particle collider, or even construct a battleship. Its small population size severely restricts its military expenditures, economic power, and thus its international position. Conversely, India, despite its greater relative poverty, can develop space technology, navies, and nuclear weapons simply because it has so many citizens that collectively they can sustain large government programs.

This difference in size and scope also affects the tenor of electoral politics: we would expect India's electoral politics not only to be more rationalized and remote than Jamaica's, but also to be even more fervently ideological, a byproduct of its greater scope. A simple comparison of the two nations' parties would seem to bear this out. India has seven national parties and hundreds of other regional parties that are highly differentiated along ideological lines, ranging from parties like the Revolutionary Socialist Party of Kerala on the left to the Bharatiya Janata Party on the right, to numerous sectarian, caste, and ethnic parties in between. Jamaica, by contrast, has only two significant political parties that are relatively closer in ideological·terms.

Larger democracies are also likely to be more biased simply because they are more likely to be heterogeneous and thus will have more members making group-based claims relative to the bigger projects their governments can pursue. Returning to our comparison of Jamaica and India, Jamaica will be less biased not only because it is relatively more affluent (its GDP per capita is four times greater than India's), but because it is less racially and ethnically diverse. Over 90 percent of Jamaica's population traces its ancestry to Africa and speaks English as its primary language. India is divided by scores of languages, religious sects, social classes, and a highly stratified caste system. Not only does India's greater diversity contribute to its incredibly large number of political parties, but these different ethnic and religious groups become power conduits of patronage politics relative to the country's larger endeavors. In fact, across countries, ethno-linguistic fractionalization is highly correlated with estimates of government corruption (Mauro 1998).

Finally, democracies that are high in scope are also likely to be more biased in their politics. As noted earlier, one characteristic of a broad-scope democracy is the extent that its power is concentrated in the hands of a unitary executive. When governing power is thus concentrated, it provides more opportunities for the entrepreneurial politician to cultivate specific political constituencies through particular contracts or decisions. Indeed, it was such concerns with this type of bias that prompted the framers of the U.S. Constitution to have the branches of government share so many powers. At a more general level, a democracy larger in scope is likely to attract more ideological groups that seek to either attenuate or exacerbate social and economic differences among residents. In a large national election, in which socialist or pro-capitalist parties participate, bias will fundamentally be about the distribution of goods and resources in a society; in a small-scope democracy there is less opportunity for making such changes and the tenor of its elections will be defined less by the specific claims of particular groups.

COMPARING AMERICAN GOVERNMENTS BY SIZE, SCOPE, AND BIAS

Together, these three characteristics can thus differentiate almost any democracy from another. Consider, for example, the range of characteristics among governmental units in the United States. Figure 1.2 is a stylized depiction of the distribution of governments by their size, scope, and bias. Along each dimension, one finds a high degree of differentiation by government type. Most municipalities and special district governments (SDGs) are on the smaller side of the size dimension, but the variance is pretty great. After all, American municipalities include towns of fewer than 500 and cities with more than 8 million. States and counties also are widely distributed along these dimensions: Vermont, Wyoming, North Dakota, and Montana have under a million residents while states like California, New York, Texas, and Florida have tens of millions

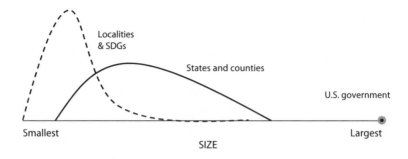

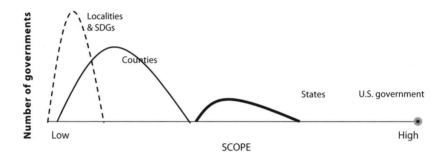

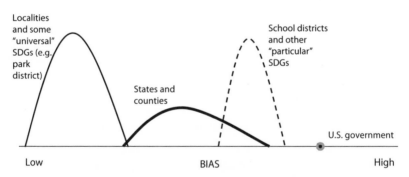

Figure 1.2. Distribution of American governments by size, scope, and bias.

and are larger than many countries. At the far end of the size spectrum is, of course, the federal government.

A similar pattern occurs by scope. States, being sovereign over local governments, will generally have more scope than any city or special district and are somewhat differentiated from each other as well, which is partly a function of their size and partly a function of their institutional arrangements (i.e., some state governments, such as California, are highly constrained by various propositions and initiatives that put caps on taxation and mandates on expenditures). Localities and special districts generally have less scope than states but are also more varied between each other. Some local governments, like New York City, have almost as much scope as states, although even the most grandiose locality will not have as much scope as the smallest state simply because localities are always subservient to state government and because most municipalities must share institutional responsibilities with their counties. Municipalities also vary in scope by the number of services they provide—cities that run airports, schools, and power authorities being greater in scope than cities that do not. Special district governments, given that they typically have a single function (such as a fire or library district) are the most narrow in scope.

The greatest amount of overlap among the various levels of government is along the bias dimension. As already noted, bias is a very difficult concept to operationalize (more on this in chapters to follow), but let us suppose that a zero score indicates a completely universal distribution of a government's goods and services and a high score would be a completely biased distribution, where all revenues are directed to one recipient. Given the highly skewed pattern of entitlement programs, state earmarks, and mildly progressive tax structure, the American federal government is probably somewhere in the mid to high range of the bias scale. Most state governments are probably less biased than the federal government, although some that are either economically stratified (e.g., Alabama or Louisiana) or highly corrupt (e.g., New Jersey and Illinois) might score higher than the federal government. The greatest variation in bias exists among localities, simply because when compared with one another, they are most varied in their income levels, racial composition, and institutional arrangements. In other words, by virtue of poverty alone, bias is going to be a lot higher in poor places like Camden, New Jersey, than in wealthy, homogeneous places like Winnetka, Illinois. Similarly, some localities, like Bell, California, or Nassau County, New York, are notorious for their corruption, which would also elevate their bias scores; meanwhile, the vast majority of suburbs, because of their "reform" style institutional arrangements and a limited menu of government services, score relatively low on the bias scale. Special district governments (SDGs) also vary widely in their bias. At the low end are general service SDGs like park and fire districts, which offer services that all constituents enjoy in near equal measure; at the other end are school districts whose high bias scores come from the fact that all residents pay school taxes even though only a portion actually use school services.[12]

Taken together, we can thus see how the electoral politics would be different between national, state, and local offices. The U.S. federal government is large in size, high in scope, and high in bias. Thus we would expect its elections to be driven by mass advertising, influenced by heuristics like party identification, more ideological, and animated by a host of interest groups looking to mobilize their supporters to defend their political prerogatives. Most municipal governments, conversely, are small in size, limited in scope, and low in bias. Their elections should be determined by more personal contacts between voters and candidates, serve as referenda on the managerial competence of incumbents, and be defined by far fewer special interest groups.

Differentiating Local Governments by Size, Scope, and Bias

Size, scope, and *bias* are useful not just for distinguishing elections between nations and localities but for appreciating the differences in electoral politics among local governments. Where a municipality or special district resides on all three dimensions will determine the nature of its electoral politics and the importance of factors like partisanship, issues, ethnic cues, or incumbency. Table 1.3 gives examples of local governments based on where they reside in size and bias and the electoral politics that are likely to exist in each place. Because most local governments are so limited in scope, these examples assume that all of these places have rela-

---

[12]Although one could argue that all of society benefits from having an educated populace or that public education is theoretically available to all residents. It is arguments such as this that make bias such a difficult concept to pinpoint.

tively low scope and are managerial democracies although, as we'll see in later chapters, local governments do exhibit some variation in this dimension as well. Nevertheless, for simplicity's sake, this example should provide a basic illustration about how the combination of the two dimensions of size and bias differentiate the electoral politics of various local governments.

The first category of democracy are those places smaller in size (i.e., under 100,000 residents) and low in bias. This would include most American municipalities and many SDGs in the United States. These are democracies that offer a limited range of "universal" public services, such as police and fire protection, waste management, street paving, and so forth. As noted earlier, in this group, local elections are based primarily on personal connections between voters and politicians. In most cases, we would expect elections to be largely referenda on incumbent performance, and revolve more around general managerial competence than any ideological issues. Most politicians run for office out of a sense of civic duty, votes are based on direct contact between politicians and voters, and voters base their decisions less on party, ideology, or even particular issues and more on their general assessment of governing performance. In such places, incumbents often run unopposed, but because political issues are likely to be parochial and idiosyncratic, it will be very difficult to predict when incumbents lose. A typical example of such a place is Kannapolis, North Carolina, a suburb of Charlotte, which has the type of politics one would find in most American towns of under 50,000 residents.

In the next category we find local governments that are small in size but high in bias. The most common type of government in this category is likely to be independent school districts although other types of SDGs, like sports complex authorities or boll weevil control districts, are likely to be included as well, particularly if they get their revenue through taxing all residents in their domain. Elections for small SDGs are likely to be based on personal connections between politicians and voters (as they will for any small government) and be concerned more with managerial competence than ideological issues (as with any organization narrow in scope). But where these elections differ from most suburban municipalities is in the effects of bias. Because there is a subset of the popula-

TABLE 1.3
How Population Size and Bias Differentiates Local Campaigns

	Low Bias	*High Bias*

Small Size	• Civic-minded politicians
	 • Personal connections
	   b/w voters and candidates
	 • Low-key campaigns
	 • Elections referenda on
	   incumbent performance
	   (Example: Kannapolis, NC)
		• Candidates arise from interest
		   groups
		 • Personal connections
		   b/w voters and candidates
		 • Mobilization of interest
		   group members
		 • Elections center on particular
		   issues and group interests
		   (Example: Rosemont, IL)

Large Size	• Ambitious candidates
	 • Large-scale campaigns
	 • Formal campaign structures
	 • Elections referenda on
	   incumbent performance
	   (Example: Garland, TX)
		• Ambitious candidates
		 • Large-scale campaigns
		 • Organizations and parties
		   active in mobilizing
		   key supporters
		 • Elections center on key issues
		   and group interests
		   (Example: Chicago, IL)

tion within these democracies getting a disproportionate share of resources, these groups will be keenly interested in sustaining their benefits: teachers' unions particularly active in school board elections, farmers turning out for boll weevil control district contests, and so on. Elections in such contests are likely to be dominated by the concerns of the particular groups. For example, union contracts, bond issues, and school closings are typically the central focus of school district elections (Moe 2005). It is possible to find a handful of small municipalities in this group that have political machines, but this is unlikely as most towns with political machines tend to be broader in scope.

There are also a few municipalities that have the unusual combination of small size and high bias. One such place is Rosemont, Illinois. Despite having only 4,200 residents, Rosemont hosts an array of facilities that would be the envy of any large city: a sprawling convention center, a 4,300-seat concert hall, and an 18,000-seat sports arena. Why does such a small town have so many facilities? They were all the brainchild of Donald Stephens, who was mayor of Rosemont from its incorporation in 1956 until his death in 2007. Stephens saw the opportunities that would be presented by the expansion of the nearby O'Hare International Airport and used these to help Rosemont grow from a tiny hamlet of 85 residents in the 1950s to its current size and stature. Throughout his tenure, Stephens dominated politics in Rosemont, responsible for hiring nearly all of employees of the town, awarding numerous contracts to build its impressive array of public amenities, and energizing the entire atmosphere of the community. Not surprisingly, Stephens maintained his control for so long by rewarding political supporters and family members, such as naming his grandson chief of police. The combination of small size, large scope, and bias is basically a recipe for an electoral politics to be dominated by a family, tribe, or close-knit ethnic group utilizing patronage to keep a hold on power.

The next group comprises places larger in size (i.e., over 100,000 in population) but low in bias. This includes a number of big cities, suburbs, and counties with limited discretionary power. A good example of such a place is the suburb of Garland, Texas. With nearly a quarter of a million residents, Garland is one of the larger municipalities in the United States, yet, in spite of its size, it hosts a very modest range of public amenities, focusing mostly on the types of services one would find an any small suburb, like roads, zoning, water, and waste service. Unlike other large cities, many of Garland's public services, such as public health and education, are administered through independent special district governments or the county. And although it has a mayor and large city council, it is effectively run by a professional city manager who is not elected. With these characteristics, electoral politics in a place like Garland are similar to the first category of democracies. In other words, they are decided less by party, ideology, or even particular issues and more by general assessments of governing performance. In fact, the only difference between a place like Garland and Kannapolis, North Carolina, would be the scale of politics. With so many residents, it would be difficult for a mayor like Garland's Ronald Jones to meet or know most voters, and so his electoral strategy must rely more on mass appeals than personal connections. But even while his style of campaigning would be different, its substance would not be too dissimilar from a smaller suburb.

The last category includes those larger places that are also high in bias. In this category we see most big cities, larger SDGs, and some county governments dominated by political machines, as in Nassau County, New York. Because of the high bias found in these places, elections would be contested by particular groups, such as teachers' unions, ethnic groups, or local political machines; but because of the larger place-size, these groups would have to engage in more mass politics. These would include more extensive advertising for candidates, holding elections at unusual times to limit turnout, and recruiting candidates who are particularly motivated by the concerns of the interest group or machine. But while these elections are likely to be more contentious, they should not have the same ideological tenor of elections in broad-scope democracies. Instead, voting would be influenced more by the mobilization of party supporters or members of particular interest groups.

CONCLUSION

Most political observers would immediately recognize that the electoral politics of a suburban municipality or a school district are going to be different than that of a big city, state, or the federal government. Yet, despite this fact, most observers habitually treat voting behavior in all types of elections as fundamentally similar. What has been missing is any kind of mechanism for systematically differentiating the electoral politics of one type of democracy from another. The characteristics of size, scope, and bias can provide just such a framework for doing this. As the examples in this chapter illustrate, identifying a democracy's size, scope, and bias allows us to make some specific predictions about its electoral politics and thus the voting behavior of its citizens.

Of course, as with any parsimonious model, such a simple account leaves out many other explanatory factors. For instance, this discussion says nothing specifically about the form of a democracy's governing institutions. Among nations, the differences between presidential and parliamentary democracies or between democracies with single-member districts versus proportional representation are substantial and greatly affect the tenor of electoral politics (Lipjhart 1999). Similarly, much research on local politics in the United States has focused on the differences between reform and nonreform style political institutions. So why are institutions not represented as a central characteristic of comparative electoral politics?

The answer is in their comparability. A democracy's institutional arrangements undoubtedly will have a profound impact on its electoral politics, but coming up with a singular metric of its institutional arrangements is nearly impossible. Consider just a few of the institutional questions a democracy must decide when constituting itself: Does it have an elected executive? Does it allow for political parties? Does it inhibit voter turnout? Does it make it difficult to run for office? Does it provide public financing of campaigns? It is simply unclear how the answers to all of these questions could be aligned along a singular continuum. Consequently, it may be more useful to simply evaluate institutional arrangements relative to the scope and bias of a democracy. In other words, does the democracy concentrate power in the hands of an executive governing board? Does the democracy's rules allow for the dispersal of selective incentives for partisan participation (i.e., does it allow of the politicization of its bias)? When comparing electoral politics across democracies, it makes more sense to appreciate institutional peculiarities relative to the dimensions of scope and bias than as a distinct category of effect.

Similarly, this discussion has said little about the importance of other social characteristics such as class, race, ethnicity, or religion, characteristics that figure so prominently in the electoral politics of many democracies. Once again, this is a deliberate choice. While the social composition of a democracy will undoubtedly affect the tenor of its political life, it is unclear how one can singularly categorize all types of democracies relative to their social makeup. Indeed, categorizing democracies relative to their social composition raises a host of intractable political questions: How important are ethnic differences versus racial ones? What is more important for class politics: income heterogeneity or wealth stratification? Should religious differences be characterized relative to a particular sect or to a general denomination?

Rather than wade through such complex issues, it is conceptually more efficient to understand the electoral implications of these social categories primarily through the lenses of size, scope and bias. After all, social diversity is probably less important in a small, narrow, and universal democracy because the connections between voters and politicians is so personal, the nature of politics so un-ideological, and political resources so non-particularistic. Class, ethnic, and religious politics are more common where politics are mass-scale, the democracy contests ideological issues, or the benefits of office can be distributed to particular groups. This is not to suggest that social characteristics are not intrinsically important to electoral politics. Even the smallest managerial democracy is likely to be affected by some type of social division. Rather, for purposes of making generalizations, it is simply more useful to appreciate their impact relative to these other traits. With these characteristics in hand, we can now examine the electoral politics of small-scale democracy in general and American local governments in particular.

CHAPTER 2

Who Votes in Local Elections?

IN THE SPRING OF 2009 only thirty-one residents of Golf, Illinois, voted in their village election. At first glance, this may seem like yet another example of the oft-heard complaint about civic apathy in the United States. Golfers, like many American citizens, were not living up to their civic responsibilities and, with such low turnout, the democratic legitimacy of their local government would be in question. In reality, however, it is unclear just how problematic this vote total actually was. Gerald Daus, the candidate elected as village president, ran unopposed and the only single vote he did not get from the thirty-one voters was for a write-in candidate. Moreover, it is not clear why anyone would run against him. In the years he had been managing village affairs, Daus had done a good job keeping the budget balanced and avoiding major tax increases. Most Golfers would appear to have been satisfied with the running of their town. So is the low electoral turnout in Golf or any other election in the United States really a sign of democratic failure?

To answer this question, we need to appreciate how deceptively slippery the concept of democracy is. The term initially appears to be quite simple: from the original Greek, "democracy" literally means rule (*kratos*) of the people (*demos*). But as one contemplates this notion, a host of difficult questions becomes apparent. Who are the people—all persons within a democracy's domain or a select few? Among these, are the people a majority, a plurality, or a unanimity? How are they to rule? Will they elect representatives or do they need to ratify each decision? Is voting sufficient to make their preferences known or must they continually express themselves by other means?

Although philosophers have been grappling with these questions since the time of Aristotle, for most contemporary democratic organizations, these normative questions are answered in a pragmatic fashion. The *demos* are the constituent members of an organization: the citizens of a nation, residents of a town, members of a union or a board, the congregants of a church, and so forth. Their primary mechanism of rule is the vote: electing governing officers or voting directly on propositions is typically seen as the most equitable and efficient mechanism for aggregating member preferences (Dahl 2000). Although there are numerous variations on how officers are elected or popular preferences aggregated (e.g., parliamentary versus presidential democracy, proportional versus district representation, majority versus plurality decisions, etc.), nearly all models of democracy utilize voting as the primary mechanism for constituent members to exercise their sovereignty.

Yet even with these pragmatic solutions, the ambiguities of democracy remain, revolving particularly around issues of electoral participation. When a democracy makes voting central to its operating logic, it faces the question of how many constituents need to vote for the group to be truly democratic. The solution may not always be straightforward. For example, in American national elections, low voter turnout is a continuing source of concern. Americans are often accused of civic laxity because their voting rates (roughly 60 percent of eligible citizens in 2008) lag so far behind their European counterparts (Powell 1986; Franklin 2004). Some even question the basic legitimacy of America's democratic institutions, particularly as so many nonvoters tend to be young, uneducated, and nonwhite (Piven and Cloward 1979).

Interestingly though, most political scientists estimate that Americans' comparatively low rates of turnout have very little impact on the outcome of national elections. Researchers find that the distribution of political preferences among nonvoters is largely similar to that of voters in presidential and congressional elections (Highton and Wolfinger 2001; Citrin, Schickler, and Sides 2003). In other words, even if every eligible citizen voted in the presidential election of 2008, Barack Obama would still have been elected by roughly the same proportion of the electorate. From a normative perspective, low voter turnout is not a problem in national elections because voters and nonvoters are not systematically dissimilar in their preferences.

But what about local elections? As in national elections, conventional wisdom would suggest that for a small-scale democracy
to be truly democratic, it too must have the most possible members take part in its elections. Once again, however, this simplistic
conception of turnout may not always hold true. The representativeness of any election will hinge on the size of the democracy,
the diversity of its members' opinions, systematic differences between voters and nonvoters, the various motivations of members
to vote, and the notion that nonvoting is an expression of real and
informed preferences. As in a national election, a lower turnout in
a local election may not be a problem depending on the conditions
just listed.

This leads us to the specific case of voter turnout in municipal
elections. If electoral turnout is low in national elections, it is especially low in local races. Turnout in most local elections, particularly when they are nonconcurrent with state or national races, is
usually below 25 percent of eligible voters and is often under 10
percent (Hajnal and Lewis 2003). At first glance, such low turnout
not only calls into question the legitimacy of local government
as a truly democratic enterprise, but also the very nature of local
politics. When only a *small* portion of the electorate votes, candidates will dramatically change the nature of their campaigns and
the strategies of their mobilization efforts; for example, candidates
would be foolhardy to spend large amounts on radio or newspaper ads if only a fraction of voters actually turn out. When only
a *particular* portion of the electorate votes, it will dramatically
change the nature of the issues that are contested in the election
and pursued by local governance. In order to understand how both
democracy and politics work in local elections, we need first to
identify both dimensions.

This chapter examines who votes in local elections and whether
their low electoral turnout is problematic for the legitimacy of
their local democracies. The evidence suggests that, for the overwhelming number of American municipalities, low turnout is not
a problem because of the types of people who vote in local contests: educated homeowners who are long-term residents of their
communities. These "homevoters" (Fischel 2001) are not only

more committed to their communities but are also more likely to be politically engaged and informed about local affairs. Although they tend to be more fiscally conservative than renters, they do not systematically differ in their opinions about all political and social issues. Whatever biases do exist as a result of low turnout in local elections are tilted toward policies that protect property values and suppress property taxes. However, given the difference in political knowledge and interest between voters and nonvoters, it is not clear that higher turnout would change this, largely because nonvoters would probably have less clearly informed preferences. Although low turnout may influence descriptive racial representation in larger and more diverse places (Hajnal and Trounstine 2005), the small size and political homogeneity of most American municipalities means that the small number of stakeholders who are voting in elections are generally articulating the sentiments of their neighbors in an effective and meaningful way. To better understand this counterintuitive sentiment, let us examine turnout relative to the characteristics of democracies described in chapter 1.

Does Low Voter Turnout Matter in a Managerial Democracy?

As with other aspects of electoral politics, the problem of low voter turnout depends largely on the size, scope, and bias of the democracy in question. In other words, the interrelated questions of "Who votes?" and "Does low turnout matter?" depend on how large a democracy is (i.e., its size), how much sovereign authority it holds (i.e., its scope) and how particularistic its programs are (i.e., its bias). Where a democratic organization sits on these dimensions will influence not only who votes but also whether low voter turnout will result in an outcome that does not mirror its constituents' preferences.

Consider the issue of size. How accurately a vote total represents the real sentiments of a particular constituency depends upon both the number of people in that constituency who vote and the diversity of sentiments they hold. In theory, voting can be like any public opinion survey that is used to estimate a population parameter. The vote total is basically a statistic, a mathematical expression of a general sentiment, and whatever inferences one draws from it depends on the bias of the estimator. In public opinion surveys, the standard error is the proportion of the variance in a population and is relative to the number of cases being sampled.[1] Standard errors increase, and the reliability of the survey results decreases, as the variance in the population grows and/or the number of cases shrinks. Moreover, these two facts are related: the greater the variance in the actual population, the more necessary it is to sample from a larger number of cases in order to generate a reliable statistic.[2] If we assume that a group of voters represent a random sample of the electorate (and more on this in a moment) then, as in any survey sample, we could accurately gauge the sentiments of a population with a relatively small percentage of voters, depending upon the heterogeneity of the population's preferences and the size of the democracy in question: the more diverse the preferences (i.e., the greater the variance), the larger the number of votes would be needed to generate a result that would, mathematically speaking, be highly unlikely to be the consequence of pure random error.

Here is where the size of a democracy comes into play. If we temporarily embrace the implausible assumption that voters represent a random sample of a democracy's constituents, then the turnout level necessary to ensure an accurate measure of popular sentiment will vary directly in relationship to the size and diversity of the democratic organization. Basically, either the larger or the less diverse the democracy, the lower the proportional turnout can be yet still provide an accurate measure of preferences. Compare, for example, three hypothetical democracies: the Very Exclusive Yacht

---

[1] This is based on the mathematics of statistics where the inferential power of a statistic (as indicated by its standard error) is calculated as the direct proportion of variance in a population relative the square root of the number of cases.

[2] Although once a sample size reaches a certain number (roughly 1000), the changes in variability of the estimates decline because of the mathematics involved in calculating standard errors. In other words, the inferential power of a statistic generated by going from 100 cases to 200 cases is far greater than going from 1000 cases to 1100 cases.

Club (500 members), the Iconoclast Society (1,000 members), and the National Fisherman Association (100,000 members). If all three clubs were electing a new president, then the importance of proportional turnout would differ greatly for each. For example, if only 5 percent of the members in each group votes in an election, it will be far more problematic for the yachters and iconoclasts than the fisherman, because a sample size of 25 and 50 will leave a much larger standard error than a sample size of 5,000. However, the small turnout may be less problematic for the yachters than the iconoclasts because the yachters' preferences are probably far more similar to one another other than the iconoclasts.

The general point is that, from the perspective of democratic theory, low turnout by itself is not necessarily problematic if a democracy is either sufficiently large or homogeneous and the voters are randomly drawn from the organization's membership base. In the context of local elections, this means that, not taking any other factors into account, the substantive impact of turnout will vary considerably according to population size of the place and the diversity of opinion within it. Low turnout in the village of Golf, Illinois (population 449), may seem like a big problem because the standard errors around a sample size of thirty-one are going to be quite high. But this may be counteracted by the fact that Golfers have a relatively uniform set of preferences with respect to local politics. In other words, the thirty Golfers who voted for Gerald Daus as village president in the 2009 election may not be any less representative of all 449 Golfers than the 465,706 Chicagoans who voted in 2007 are representative of all 2.8 million Chicagoans —Golfers are probably a lot more homogeneous in their political preferences than Chicagoans are. Indeed, the fact that Daus ran unopposed suggests that the electorate was probably not very politically divided or upset with his tenure as village president.

Of course, the above discussion has a major problem: voters rarely represent a random sample of eligible citizens for the simple reason that some types of people are more likely to vote than others. Thus the representativeness of any local election will hinge on two questions: Who is likely to vote? And, do voters accurately represent the diversity of political opinion within a population? Together, these two questions are difficult to answer because they are so interrelated. Take the example of senior citizens in presidential elections. In national elections, older and more educated citizens are far more likely to cast ballots than the young and less educated (Wolfinger and Rosenstone 1980). And while political scientists may claim that turnout doesn't affect electoral outcomes, the concerns of senior citizens remain paramount in any presidential campaign (Campbell 2005). Not only are national elections less likely to be representative if seniors are more likely to vote, but also candidates will position themselves to attract senior citizen votes. In other words, the population characteristic in question (people's electoral preferences) is endogenous to the mechanism of measuring it (the vote), thus reducing our confidence in the accuracy of the statistic.

So to understand whatever biases may lurk in low turnout, we need to first identify who is most likely to vote. From the voluminous literature on turnout in national elections, a fairly simple answer has been found that is probably applicable to any democratic organization: the people who turn out to vote are those who are more intrinsically motivated, extrinsically mobilized, or differentially affected by the costs of voting (Wolfinger and Rosenstone 1980; Verba, Schlozman, and Brady 1995). The intrinsically motivated are those with the most financial, social, or psychological stakes involved in the outcome of the election. Such "stakeholders" could be those members who derive greater benefits from their membership or whose identity or well-being is directly tied to the democracy's future. Stakeholders can come in many forms: they can be senior citizens concerned with the future of social security; they can be party workers whose jobs depend on keeping a political machine in power; they can be lifelong members of a club who get most of their social interaction from an organization; they can be stockholders with a large financial investment in a company; they could even be avid viewers of *American Idol* with a strong emotional tie to a certain contestant. Who turns out to vote will depend a lot on the material, psychological, or social attachments of the voters to the outcome.

Voter participation will also be shaped by extrinsic factors, particularly the efforts of certain candidates or groups to mobilize their supporters. Strategic candidates who run for office in a democratic organization not only tailor their campaign messages toward stakeholders, but try to mobilize any voters who are sympathetic to their views. In both national and local elections, scholars have found that mobilization efforts make a tremendous difference in turnout levels and the types of people who are more likely to vote (Gerber, Green, and Larimer, 2008). For example, looking at national data from the 1970s and 1980s, political scientists Steven Rosenstone and Mark Hansen (1993) found that most of the declines in national voter turnout were due to declining levels of mobilization. Americans were voting less in presidential elections in these two decades because fewer candidates and party organizations were asking them to do so. These mobilization effects are likely to occur in any type of democratic organization and may arise formally from orchestrated efforts of candidates or informally through social networks and peer pressure (Gerber et al. 2008).

Beyond the intrinsic motivations and extrinsic mobilizations, there is another important factor that affects who votes: the costs of voting. Political scientists are often fond of explaining voting behavior relative to the costs and benefits each citizen experiences from electoral participation (Downs 1957; Riker and Ordershook 1968). Although the benefits of voting have proven to be an elusive quarry (particularly since they seem to be so ineffable), the costs of voting have been easy to demonstrate. Several studies have convincingly shown that reducing the costs of elections, such as by facilitating voter registration or publicizing election dates, greatly increases voter turnout (Highton 1997). So when and how organizations hold their elections will make a large impact on turnout. Because voting is costly, turnout will naturally be skewed toward members with greater skills or resources. Indeed, one reason why education is such a strong predictor of voting turnout in national elections is because the more educated putatively have greater resources and skills for clearing the various hurdles (e.g., registration, identifying polling places, remembering election dates, etc.) involved in voting (Wolfinger and Rosenstone 1980).

In short, with any democratic organization, answering the question of "who votes?" depends on identifying the "stakeholders," what the candidates or campaigns are doing to mobilize them, and the costs of voting. Here is where the other two dimensions that differentiate democratic organizations (scope and bias) are quite useful, for the types of stakeholders and the pressures to mobilize will vary systematically in regard to each of these dimensions. Specifically, *as a democracy narrows in scope, the population of stakeholders becomes increasingly small; as a democracy grows more biased, the variance in preferences among members becomes much greater.*

These assertions can be easily demonstrated by comparing the example of three elections: the president of the United States, a school board president, and the president of a local garden club. Most Americans have a strong incentive to vote in their presidential election, not just because of the material consequences of a presidential administration, but because of the symbolic and existential qualities embodied in the office. As the *de facto* leader of the nation as well as the head of the state, the president represents who Americans are as a people. With regards to school board elections, the stakes are much more concentrated among parents of school-aged children than nonparents but sometimes senior citizens (wary of property tax increases and not receiving direct benefits of good schools) may also join in the fray. Yet, by and large, the range of stakeholders is much smaller than for the national election. In the garden club election, it is unclear who is more invested in its outcome, but it would probably be long-time club members or active participants in club activities and would represent an even smaller fraction of the membership.

In addition to its scope, the amount of bias in a democratic organization will also skew material incentives toward voter turnout. Bias, as described in chapter 1, refers to the distribution of costs and benefits across its entire constituency. The greater the bias in a democracy (i.e., the more disproportionately it distributes its collective goods to a narrow group), the greater the incentive to vote among the beneficiaries of the democracy's largess. Consider again the three examples from above. The American government is heavily biased in its spending toward senior citizens—roughly 42 percent of the federal budget goes to programs for senior citizens, specifically Social Security and Medicare. Given the financial stakes, seniors' higher turnout rates are thus not surprising. In fact, political scientist Andrea Campbell (2005) finds that disproportionate senior citizen turnout developed only after social security and Medicare were both instituted. Similarly, school district spending is something that only parents of school-aged children benefit from, thus it is not surprising that they vote in disproportionately higher numbers for school board elections (Howell 2005). We might even expect to see turnout differences in the garden club if certain members were receiving special benefits that were not made available to all.

Consequently, the scope and bias of an organization will determine not only who votes but how they vote and, thus, the representativeness of a low turnout election. Scope and bias, however, have very different implications for low turnout. As noted in chapter 1, when a democracy diminishes in scope, its governance grows more managerial in character. Returning to the earlier example, the national presidential election, being for the office with the highest scope in the country, will engender a wide range of existential questions. By contrast, most school board elections will not deal with issues of foreign policy or even fundamental philosophies of governance even if they still encompass some ideological issues such as those raised by the teaching of sexual education or evolution. Typically though, school board elections are more focused on management issues such as teacher pay and infrastructure improvements (Howell 2005). The garden club election is unlikely to hold any ideological significance and will most likely be simply about who is willing to balance the books and make administrative decisions. Thus, ceteris paribus, the more narrow in scope an organization, the more managerial it becomes as a democracy, and the less likely that low turnout will be less representative (and normatively problematic), simply because there are fewer divisive issues that could separate the preferences of voters. In other words, *the more limited the powers of a democracy, the less likely its constituents will have strong or irreconcilable preferences, and the less problematic low turnout will be.*

Bias in a democracy, by contrast, will directly impinge on the representativeness of turnout in an election. In a biased democracy, preferences are relatively easy to track—people who disproportionately benefit will typically have different preferences than those who do not. If we assume that beneficiaries of a biased democracy are more likely to vote because of their greater material incentives, low turnout in elections will yield a less representative picture of overall constituent preferences. Although the substantive magnitude of an organization's bias will change with its scope (bias in a nation-state has far greater ramifications than bias in a garden club), the dimension of bias should generally be seen as orthogonal to the dimension of scope and can occur in any type of a democracy. This is because bias generally refers to the particular distribution of certain organizational resources and typically does not involve ideological matters. Thus, no matter its scope, the greater a democracy's bias (or potential for bias), the more problematic low turnout will be, since beneficiaries of the bias are not only the most likely to vote but will also seek to retain the patronage of their elected representatives.

Finally, biases arising from low voter turnout will be exacerbated by the costs of voting. When voting is more costly, the beneficiaries of the bias are going to be that much more likely to turn out and this difference will magnify the unrepresentativeness of the vote. Returning to our three examples, we see that the costs of voting typically increase as the scope and bias of an organization decreases. Presidential elections are very well publicized and occur at regularized intervals. There are also numerous statutes, such as the motor voter provision, that attempt to facilitate registration, and most jurisdictions send out reminder cards of when national elections are occurring. This is not the case with school board elections, which are often scheduled for odd or unusual times precisely in order to reduce voter turnout. Elections in civic organizations, like a garden club, are typically even more obscure and may occur in an ad hoc fashion. Interestingly, as the scope of an organization decreases or as its biases increase, the costs of voting will usually rise, thus further accentuating differences among the interested, mobilized, and skilled.

In sum, for all democracies, be they nation states or garden clubs, low electoral turnout is problematic only to the extent that voters are unrepresentative of the general membership. Such unrepresentativeness is more likely to occur as democracies become smaller, more heterogeneous in membership, greater in their institutional power, and more biased in the distribution of their resources. Considering the entire universe of democratic organizations, low turnout will be most normatively problematic in a small, diverse, and corrupt nation-state (e.g., Lebanon) and less so in a large, homogeneous, universalistic, and narrow organization (e.g., a mosquito abatement district in an affluent suburban area). In short, the problem of low turnout is largely relative to the particular type of democracy in question.

Does Low Voter Turnout Matter in Local Elections?

With this framework in hand, we can now turn our attention to local elections. As noted previously, turnout in local elections is usually below 35 percent of eligible voters and can be much lower depending on when the election is held and which offices are at stake. Consider some aggregate findings listed in table 2.1. Looking at a sample of 492 municipal elections over three time periods from a selection of twenty-eight counties in fifteen states, a substantial variation occurs in electoral turnout depending on when the election is held.[3] When local elections are concurrent with national elections, there is a very high rate of voter participation:

---

[3] There are no reliable aggregate datasets that examine local turnout rates across the country. For this research, we tabulated results from 492 municipalities in fifteen states for elections in 2004, 2005, and 2006. Although this is not a purely random sample, it is sufficiently diverse in terms of size, racial composition, and income to provide a reasonable accurate picture of differences in local turnout rates, particularly in comparing off-year and concurrent elections.

Table 2.1
Statistics on Voter Turnout in Local Elections 2004–2006

Variable	Mean	Standard Deviation	Minimum	Median	Maximum
Turnout in 2006 (%)	50.3	16.2	2.0	53.5	80.8
Concurrent Election	55.6	9.1	30.1	55.0	80.0
Nonconcurrent Election	18.3	12.0	2.0	15.0	47.9
Turnout in 2005 (%)	35.0	18.2	0.8	38.5	95.4
Turnout in 2004 (%)	70.6	16.7	6.1	76.1	89.1
Concurrent Election	76.4	6.0	60.4	77.2	89.1
Nonconcurrent Election	32.6	14.9	6.1	32.5	65.8

Source: Sample of 492 municipalities from twenty-eight counties in fifteen states. Specific data available from authors.

the average turnout rate among the places sampled was 76 percent during the presidential election year of 2004 and 56 percent during the congressional elections of 2006. However, when local elections are held in off-years or are nonconcurrent with national elections, the numbers drop significantly. The average turnout rate among places having local elections in 2005 was 35 percent, a number that is somewhat higher because many of these races were concurrent with elections for state offices. When local elections are held on their own, as with nonconcurrent elections in 2006, the average turnout drops to 18 percent.

But while American municipalities show dramatic differences in turnout, particularly when they are not coincidental with national elections, it is not clear whether this is normatively problematic or how it might shape voting behavior. In other words, is an 18 percent turnout in a local election held in April of 2006 any less valid than a 71 percent turnout rate in November of 2004? The only way to answer this question is to examine voter turnout relative to the characteristics of size, scope, and bias. So let us look at municipal elections relative to these characteristics.

Size and Local Turnout

American municipalities encompass a wide variety of places by way of population size. Immediately outside of Chicago, for example, municipalities can be as small as Indian Creek (population 211) and as large as Elgin (population 93,895). As noted in this book's introduction, the overwhelming majority of American municipalities are actually under 5,000 in population—many are very small, rural towns. But while most American towns are under 5,000 in size, most of the American population lives in places larger than that. Thus, for the places that most Americans live in, turnout would not have to be very high to give a relatively accurate picture of citizen preferences, if voters are a random sample of their populations. For example, in a community of 5,000 eligible voters, a 20 percent turnout rate would give a sample of 1,000 voters, which would generate a result with a very small standard error even with a high level of diversity in citizen preferences. Thus, in the vast number of communities where most Americans live, low voter turnout may not be problematic if we think that voters represent a random sample of the voting eligible population. In other words, because over 75 percent of Americans live in municipalities over 5,000 in size, the average turnout rate of 20 percent that most municipalities exhibit is not necessarily a problem, if these voters are representative of their communities.

This, however, brings up the most important question: how much confidence do we have that the people who turn out to vote in local elections are generally representative of their neighbors' preferences? This is a very tricky question, for while estimating a democracy's population size is very straightforward, estimating the diversity of its members' preferences is not. This is partly because the concept of diversity itself is so prosaic. Diversity can refer to almost any characteristic within a population, from height to favorite ice cream flavor. Furthermore, there is a matter of strength of preference. For instance, I may like chocolate ice cream while my neighbor prefers vanilla, but my neighbor may also be perfectly happy with chocolate if vanilla was not available. So when it comes to gauging the representativeness of elections, we need to anticipate what are the possible fissures on which citizens may be divided and how strong is the gap in their preferences. To this, we can look at the factors of scope and bias.

Scope and Local Turnout

Inquiries into the size and diversity of a population assume, of course, that local voters are randomly drawn from their populations. But is this the case? And, if not, who is voting in these places? As already noted, the answer to this question could come by identifying which citizens are more motivated or mobilized to vote than others, in other words, by identifying the stakeholders in local politics. According to economist William Fischel (2005), the stakeholders in local elections are very easy to identify: homeowners. Home equity value is the single largest private asset that Americans hold (eleven times larger than any liquid assets) and homeowners are keenly interested in protecting their investments. As a result, homeowners are particularly attuned to issues of local governance, especially as they relate to their property values. They will follow the decisions of locally elected leaders and take a keen interest in the economic well-being of their communities. This also means they will be very concerned with issues of zoning, taxes, services, and development, largely because these issues bear directly on the value of their single largest investment. Property owners become vigilant monitors of public affairs and rather than "voting with their feet," as other economists would suggest, they work to actively influence government to be an agent on their behalf. Fischel argues that voters will even support tax increases if such a measure will help bolster property values over the long haul. The stakeholders in local elections are, to use his term, "homevoters."

Fischel's hypothesis dovetails nicely with another important aspect of both local politics and low turnout in democratic organizations: the limited scope of local government. As noted earlier, the scope of a democracy is quite important for evaluating the representativeness of turnout. Democracies that are narrow in scope require fewer voters to represent their members' preferences because there are fewer issues that could divide the populace. As noted in chapter 1, municipal governments are bureaucratic creations of state government and are quite limited in the types of policies they can pursue by both statute and circumstance. Most localities, in order to sustain their municipal autonomy, must make provisions for certain types of services such as fire and police protection, waste treatment, and road maintenance. These mandates absorb a large amount of financial resources and, barring significant tax increases, constrain discretionary policy initiatives. Competitive pressures from surrounding municipalities will also force many localities to reduce taxes and focus more on policies that protect and enhance property values (Peterson 1981; Logan and Molotch 1987). As a result, municipal governments will not just be narrow in scope but have strong inherent pressures to focus their concerns around property issues. In other words, municipal governments are narrowly concerned with questions of land usage.

It is important to note that this discussion is concerned primarily with smaller *municipal* government. There are numerous other local governments, particularly special districts or large cities, that may have slightly different electoral dynamics. Most special district governments tend to be even narrower in scope than municipalities and thus have stakeholders that are even fewer in numbers. For example, many states have mosquito abatement districts, which are special governmental authorities set up to spray and control for mosquitoes. In short, their sole purpose is simply eradicating mosquitoes. Such governments typically have elected boards who oversee their staff, operations, and budgets, including the issuance of bonds and tax collection. But with such a narrow scope, it is hard to identify a group of stakeholders because everyone benefits equally from having fewer mosquitoes. Most likely, the stakeholders will be limited to the employees and families of employees who are contracted by the district to eradicate mosquitoes. As special districts grow wider in scope, they are likely to garner more stakeholders. Stakeholders of school districts are parents and school employees, stakeholders of water reclamation districts are property developers and environmentalists, and so on. Although the focus of this book is on municipal elections, we mention these examples only to note that not all government issues

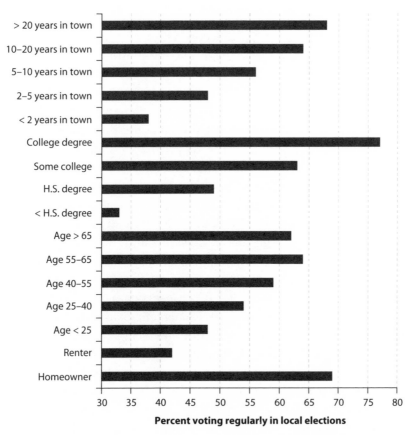

Figure 2.1. Percent regularly voting in local elections by length of residence, education, age, and homeownership. *Source*: 1990 American Citizen Participation Study.

arise from property concerns, and that stakeholders may come in many varieties depending on the type of government in question.

Nevertheless, when we consider the substantial incentives of homeowners to protect property values and the statutory incentives of municipal governments to focus on land issues, it is not surprising that the most decisive factor in determining who votes in most *municipal* elections will be their relationship to property. The importance of homeownership for local voting is evident in survey data. Figure 2.1 depicts the percent of respondents from places under 100,000 in population from the 1990 American Citizen Participation Study (ACPS) who report voting in "most" or "all" local elections, grouped according to four individual characteristics: length of residence in their communities, education, age, and homeownership.[4]

For voting in local elections, the impact of homeownership is as great as education and larger than age, which happen to be the two biggest predictors of turnout in national contests. Only 40 percent of renters in this portion of the ACPS sample reported regularly voting in local elections compared to nearly 70 percent of homeowners.[55] This difference between renters and homeowner is larger than that between age groups (fifteen percentage points between the youngest and oldest adults) and nearly as large as the turnout differences between high school dropouts and those with a college degree (44 percentage points). In fact, homeownership probably is even a more decisive predictor of overall turnout than education because high school dropouts make up such a small fraction of the adult population (less than 13 percent of the ACPS survey), whereas renters comprise nearly 35 percent. Consequently, the overall magnitude of homeownership in relationship to local turnout is probably greater than even education, traditionally the most robust predictor of electoral participation. Furthermore, also in accordance with Fischel's hypotheses, length of residence is a very decisive predictor of turnout: respondents in the ACPS who had lived in their community for more than twenty years were twice as

---

[4] The 1990 American Citizen Participation Study is a large-scale, two-stage survey of a random sample of Americans conducted in 1989 and 1990. In the second stage, the data used for this chapter came from longer in-person interviews that were conducted with 2,517 respondents. To measure their social contexts, I extracted information on both city- and metropolitan-level social characteristics from the 1990 U.S. Census. For a full description of the data, see Verba, Schlozman, and Brady 1995. Although these data are twenty years old, they remain the best data source on the participatory behaviors of the American population and are one of a few data sources that ask about voting in local elections. The dichotomous measure of local turnout was taken from the following item: "Now, thinking about the local elections that have been held since you were old enough to vote, have you voted in all of them, most of them, in some of them, rarely voted in them, or have you never voted in a local election?" Although this item does not ask them about their specific locality, it nevertheless should be an approximate gauge of local electoral participation.

[5] Similar differences can be found in other datasets that ask about voting in local elections, such as the General Social Survey.

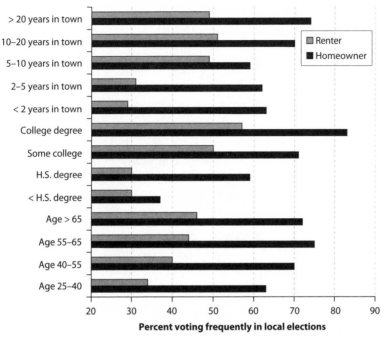

Figure 2.2. Differences in voting between homeowners and renters by length of residence, education, and age. *Source*: 1990 American Citizen Participation Study.

likely to report regularly voting in local elections than people who had lived there for less than two years.

Of course, from these simple statistics, it is difficult to know to what extent the effects of age, education, and residential length alone are important for shaping turnout and to what extent they may simply be predictors of homeownership. This point is important to consider because it can tell us how much turnout in local elections is being driven by "homevoters" as opposed to other types of stakeholders (i.e., people with social or emotional investments in their communities). A simple way of comparing these factors is by examining the self-reported local voting patterns between homeowners and renters by length of residence, education, and age.

As depicted in figure 2.2, the only factor that has a strong relationship to turnout independent of homeownership is education. For example, the differences in the self-reported voting patterns between renters and homeowners do not change across age categories. In other words, the turnout differences between young and old renters are relatively small compared to the differences between homeowners and renters across all age categories. The same holds for length of residence, except among new residents who rent, but even the newest homeowners report voting far more regularly than long-term renters. In fact, the only factor that appears to have an equivalent effect on turnout is education. Homeowners who did not finish high school report voting much less than homeowners in other categories; meanwhile renters who have a college degree report voting at rates that are comparable to homeowners with a high school degree.

The importance of homeownership and education highlight two important aspects of voting in local elections: intrinsic motivations and the costs of voting. If Fischel's "homevoter" hypothesis is correct, then homeowners are much more likely to vote in local elections because they are highly motivated to protect their home values and thus monitor local government through local elections. However, the large differences in turnout by education also suggest that other factors beyond mere "homevoting" may also be at work and that all home*owners* are not necessarily "home*voters*." One of these factors may be civic skills. Education is believed to have such a strong correlation with turnout in national elections not just because the educated tend to be more interested in politics but also because they experience lower costs of participation (Verba et al. 1995). For example, voter registration, cognizance of election dates, and locating polling places are putatively easier for the more educated as they have greater skills and experience in dealing with such bureaucratic matters.

In local elections as well, educated citizens may be more likely to vote because they are both more engaged by public affairs and because voting is less costly for them. Evidence for both of these propositions is abundant (Campbell 2009; Dee 2004; Wolfinger and Rosenstone 1980). Indeed, the intrinsic motivation of the educated and homeowners to participate in local elections is evident in the ACPS survey data about the respondents' interest in local politics. Not surprisingly, regular voters were a lot more interested

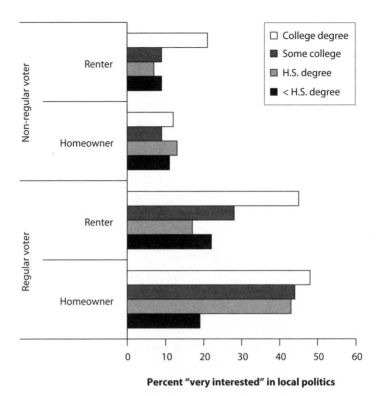

Figure 2.3. Percent very interested in local politics by homeownership, voting patterns, and education. *Source*: 1990 American Citizen Participation Study.

in local politics: 41 percent reported being very interested in local politics compared to less than 10 percent of nonregular voters.

But these aggregate differences hide some sharp distinctions between education and homeownership as factors behind voting. Figure 2.3 reports the percent of respondents who said they were very interested in local politics, across three categories: home-ownership, regular voting, and education levels. Among nonregular voters, there are few differences in political interest by either homeownership or education.[6] Among regular voters, however, there were strong differences in political interest by education, al-

---

[6] Only college-educated renters showed slightly higher average levels of political interest (a very small portion of the sample).

though this varied between renters and homeowners. For home-owners with at least a high school degree, there are only small differences in average levels of political interest, but among renters, education correlates quite strongly with political interest—roughly 45 percent of renters with a college degree who are regular voters said they were very interested in local politics, a level on par with homeowners. In short, among regular voters, homeownership seems to compensate for low levels of education in driving citizens' political interests.

Although home ownership is not the only factor that drives interest in local politics and motivates people to vote, it is easily the most important one. Among regular voters, it is the home-owners that, regardless of their education, demonstrate the highest levels of interest in local politics. But among renters, it is only the most educated who turn out in numbers comparable to the home-owning portion of the population. Given that the percent of citizens who are highly educated and rent their domiciles is quite small (under 5 percent of the population), in the aggregate it is the portion of homeowners interested in local politics who constitute the bulk of voters.

Homeownership is also important for local elections because it makes citizens more likely to be mobilized by local political campaigns. If mobilization is important for national elections, it is especially so in local ones. In a set of innovative field experiments, political scientists Alan Gerber and Donald Green found that voters who were directly contacted by an individual canvasser were far more likely to vote in local elections than those who were not (Green and Gerber 2008). These differences were greater in magnitude than those found by Rosenstone and Hansen (1993) for national elections. As we'll see in chapter 3, the overwhelming majority of local politicians engage in some type of voter mobilization effort as part of their political campaigns.

These mobilization patterns exacerbate the impact of education and homeownership because these factors also correspond with who is contacted by political campaigns. For example, in the 2008 American National Elections Studies, 48 percent of homeowners reported being urged to vote by a political campaign compared

nonvoters have a strong set of preferences relative to the various candidates' positions or ballot issues before them.

But in political life generally, and local politics in particular, this is a highly questionable assumption. Politics is a remote and distant concern for most citizens and the majority of Americans have largely unstable and ill-formed political preferences, even for large national issues (Converse 1964; Delli Carpini and Keeter 1997). Nor do they usually have a clear idea about candidate policy positions (Gilens 2001). As the scope of government diminishes, it is even less likely that most citizens will have considered and long-standing alternative preferences, because exposure to political information becomes less common. Indeed, this is one of the central factors that divide stakeholders from non-stakeholders: stakeholders are far more likely to have consistent and strong preferences about an organization than non-stakeholders. So the question regarding local turnout is not simply whether homeowners and the educated have different preferences from renters and the uneducated, but rather if the latter even have stable or clearly understood preferences to begin with.

Although the issue of information, preference, and candidate position will be taken up in more detail in chapter 5, for now it is worth examining whether the educated and homeowners have any systemically different levels of political knowledge that differentiates them from nonvoters. There are good reasons for suspecting that they do, as it is a well-documented fact that the greater a person's education, the more political information they generally know (Delli Carpini and Keeter 1997). The same also appears to be the case for homeownership. Respondents in the ACPS were asked two questions about their political knowledge: which party controlled the House of Representatives and what was the age that citizens could vote. Fifty-six percent of the respondents could answer both questions correctly, although these results differed dramatically by education: only 27 percent of high school dropouts could answer both correctly compared to 73 percent of college graduates. Similarly, 63 percent of homeowners could answer both questions correctly compared to only 45 percent of renters.

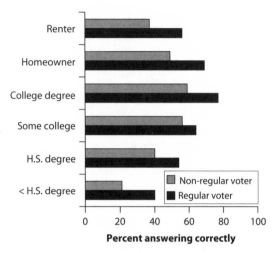

Figure 2.5. Political knowledge by voting behavior, education, and homeowner-ship. *Source*: 1990 American Citizen Participation Study.

These differences grow in magnitude, however, when comparisons are also made between regular and nonregular voters. Figure 2.5 lists the percent of respondents in the ACPS who answered both political knowledge questions correctly by homeownership and education level for both regular and nonregular voters. Although political knowledge increases with education for both groups, there is a substantial gap in the political knowledge between voters and nonvoters at every level of education. For instance, 40 percent of high school dropouts who are regular voters can answer the political knowledge questions correctly compared to only 20 percent of dropouts who are nonregular voters and 40 percent of high school graduates who also don't vote regularly. In fact, being a regular voter is roughly equivalent to one unit of education in a four-point education scale in predicting a respondent's political knowledge. Similarly, the higher political knowledge of homeowners was mediated somewhat by their voting behavior: renters who reported being regular voters were actually more knowledgeable, on average, than homeowners who were nonregular voters. Although these questions of political knowledge pertain to national politics, it is difficult to imagine that similar differences would not also be evident with respect to local affairs.

So not only do homeowners and the more educated show greater interest in politics, they also demonstrate a greater knowledge about political facts. If having a fundamental grasp of political information is essential for actually having meaningful political preferences, then these results would suggest that one of the biggest differences between voters and nonvoters is not simply that they have different preferences, but whether both groups even have political preferences at all. Given the lower levels of basic political knowledge among the less educated and renting nonvoting population, one may question whether they actually have stable or well-reasoned preferences about larger political issues. Indeed, their nonparticipation in local elections may itself be an indicator of their indecisive political preferences: not knowing much about candidates or the issues facing their communities, uninformed citizens may not have strong opinions about local politics and thus have no decisive preferences to express.

Of course, one might argue that while nonvoters have less knowledge about basic political facts or less interest in politics, it does not automatically mean that they have less defined political preferences. It may simply be that their preferences are not represented in the choices before them and, feeling disenfranchised, they simply opt out of the political process. This understandable objection, however, assumes that we can identify what types of distinct preferences nonvoters (i.e., who are disproportionately less educated and non-homeowning) might have.

Here, once again, we might gain some insights from the theories listed earlier. According to Fischel's "homevoter hypothesis," homeownership is instrumental for defining political preferences. Because homeowners have such a great financial stake in their property, they presumably are motivated to preserve and enhance their equity. Such financial considerations presumably frame their preferences toward lower taxes, property-enhancing regulations on building and development, and support for certain public services (such as public education) that have positive externalities for the housing market. Renters, by contrast, have none of these incentives and presumably would want to extract more services and amenities from local government regardless of their impact on property values. Although homeowners also seek some "use value" from their properties, the more quantifiable metric of their home's "exchange value" presumably makes them prefer policies that enhance economic growth and property value, even at the expense of some public service amenities.

Survey data demonstrate that, outside of large cities, homeowners have a set of fiscal preferences distinct from their renting counterparts. Respondents to the ACPS were asked a series of questions about national and local government spending policies and social issues.[7] Although these questions do not ask about a number of specific local government initiatives, they should capture both respondents' general fiscal priorities as well as their orientation toward local social initiatives. Table 2.2 reports the average scores on these issue position scales by homeownership and education

[7] Questions for each of the items were as follows: Government spending: Some people feel that the government should provide fewer services, even in areas such as health and education in order to reduce spending. (Suppose these people are at one end of the scale at point number 1.) Other people feel it is important for the government to provide many more services even if it means an increase in spending. (Suppose these people are at the other end, at point 7.) And, of course, some other people would have opinions somewhere in between (at points 2,3,4,5, and 6). Where would you place yourself on this scale? No Job Help: Some people feel that the government in Washington should see to it that every person has a job and a good standard of living. (Suppose these people are at one end of the scale at point number 1.) Others think that the government should just let each person get ahead on his or her own. (Suppose these people are at the other end at point 7.) And of course, some other people have opinions somewhere in between (at points 2,3,4,5, or 6). Where would you place yourself on this scale? No Religion in Public Schools: Some people think public schools should be allowed to start each day with a prayer. (Suppose these people are at one end of the scale at point number 1.) Others feel that religion does not belong in the public schools but should be taken care of by the family and the church. (Suppose these people are at the other end, at point 7.) And, of course, some other people would have opinions somewhere in between (at points 2,3,4,5, and 6). Where would you place yourself on this scale? Never Permit Abortion. Some people feel that a woman should always be able to obtain an abortion as a matter of personal choice. (Suppose these people are at one end of the scale at point number 1.) Others feel that, by law, abortions should never be permitted. (Suppose these people are at the other end, at point 7.) And, of course, some other people would have opinions somewhere in between (at points 2,3,4,5, and 6). Where would you place yourself on this scale? Gay Book Ban{. There are always some people whose ideas are considered bad or dangerous by other people. Consider someone who is openly homosexual. If some people in your community suggested that a book he or she wrote in favor of homosexuality should be taken out of your public library, would you favor removing this book or not?

TABLE 2.2
Attitudinal Differences on Social and Economic Policies by Education and
Homeownership

	Increase Govt. Govt. Spending	No Job from Government	No Religion in Public Schools	Never Permit Abortion	Percent Favor Gay Book Ban
Renter	4.7 (1.7)	3.8 (1.8)	3.6 (2.4)	3.1 (2.3)	24%
Homeowner	4.2 (1.7)	4.3 (1.7)	3.6 (2.4)	3.2 (2.3)	26%
< H.S. Degree	4.9 (2.0)	3.6 (2.1)	3.0 (2.3)	4.2 (2.5)	39%
H.S. Degree	4.4 (1.7)	4.2 (1.8)	3.2 (2.3)	3.4 (2.3)	32%
Some College	4.3 (1.7)	4.2 (1.7)	3.7 (2.4)	3.1 (2.3)	24%
College Deg.	4.2 (1.6)	4.3 (1.5)	4.3 (2.4)	2.6 (2.0)	13%

Source: 1990 American Citizen Participation Study; standard deviations are in parentheses.

for the nonurban portion of the sample. Both renters and the less educated express far greater support for increasing government spending to aid the poor and to provide job training and assistance. For instance, renters average nearly a half point in difference from homeowners on the seven-point scale for both items; high school dropouts average a seven-tenths point difference from college graduates on the same scale (although the higher standard deviations among renters and the less educated also indicate much greater variance in the opinion positions of these groups as well, which may also be a byproduct of not having firm opinions). Although not depicted here, there are no differences in these rates between regular and nonregular voters. In other words, with regard to government spending policies, the differences in preferences between homeowners and renters are no different among regular and nonregular voters for these categories. Nevertheless, renters and the less educated (particularly those without a high school degree) have much more liberal attitudes about government social spending than homeowners and the more educated.

A much different set of trends exists with respect to social policy. When comparing attitudes toward religion in public schools, abortion, or removing books from public libraries by gay authors, there are no significant differences in attitudes between homeowners and renters. Even though renters have far more liberal views about government spending, they do not have more liberal views about government social policies. Comparing attitudes by education, we find that high school dropouts express far more conservative views than those with college degrees. Not only did dropouts average more than a one-point difference on the school religion and abortion scales than college graduates, they were also three times more likely to favor banning books by gay authors from the public library. It should be noted, however, that these mean scores have much higher standard deviations than found with the mean scores on economic policy. This indicates that a much greater variance exists regarding opinions on social issues than economic ones. Once again, however, there are no systematic differences in these results if we further break down these categories by self-reported voting patterns. In other words, nonvoting renters are no less conservative on social issues than renters who vote regularly.

Conclusion

The results of this chapter suggest that in most local elections, low voter turnout is not a threat to the health, legitimacy, or representativeness of local democratic institutions. At first glance, this conclusion may come as a shock. After all, it violates many long-held assumptions about democracy in the United States. Most Americans are taught from an early age about the importance of voting as a civic duty and that voting is essential for ensuring the vibrancy of American democracy. "Voter turnout," according to a typical example from the Center for Voting and Democracy's online mission statement, "is a fundamental quality of fair elections and is generally considered to be a necessary factor for a healthy democracy."[8] It is almost a reflexive notion that higher turnout will ensure a more legitimate democratic process.

[8] Online at www.fairvote.org, accessed May 10, 2011.

Yet, with regard to most local elections, low turnout may not be the delegitimizing blight we reflexively suppose it to be. This is due to several key facts about local democracy. First, in most localities, there is a much more limited range of issues that can divide the population than one might find in states or nations. This is due to the narrow scope and relatively unbiased character of most municipalities. If elections are about expressing the preferences of the citizenry, then the range of those preferences are going to be fundamentally determined by the scope of the offices in question. Because the powers of most municipalities are so circumscribed by state mandates, there simply are fewer issues that could spark outrage or divisions among their members. For example, if the only responsibilities for a town's government are funding the fire department, paving the streets, and getting the garbage picked up, there are not going to be as many venues for ideological conflict or partisan bickering as when a democracy is fielding armies, taxing income, and determining basic political rights. This fact may also be why so many local elections go uncontested—the parameters of local governance do not usually generate chronic or long-standing cleavages in the population.

The homogeneity of citizen preferences is also attributable to the relatively unbiased character of many municipal governments. When a democracy is biased, we can expect a greater gulf in the preferences among citizens: the elderly have different opinions about Medicare and Social Security benefits than people in their twenties; the rich have different ideas about welfare payments than the poor; and so on. Although political patronage and favoritism are likely to exist in any democracy, the relative scale of such practices in most small municipalities is likely to be quite low. There are, however, two groups of local elections where bias is likely to be quite high: school board elections and places with larger commercial investments. Because independent school districts are very biased governments, low turnout is going to be more problematic for gauging citizen preferences. In other words, if I have no children or my children are grown, I will have little material incentive to support expensive bond measures or tax increases to improve school quality. Similarly, low turnout may also undermine citizen interests where large commercial interests have strong financial stakes in municipal decisions. A bond referendum for a stadium, for instance, may be supported by sports fans and will be a financial boost to team owners but will be costly to most citizens in a region (Danielson 1976).

The second reason why low turnout may be less problematic in local elections comes from the differences in the types of people who participate. Local elections are dominated by homeowners, the educated, and long-term residents—people who have strong emotional and material connections to their communities. These voters tend to exemplify all that we expect in a classical notion of the ideal democratic citizen: they are politically engaged, knowledgeable, and have definitive preferences about local policies. If all citizens voted in local elections, it is unclear whether higher turnout would improve the communication of their wishes, because so many citizens are too ignorant about local affairs to have clear opinions on public matters. They may want low crime, paved streets, fewer taxes, and better services (who wouldn't?), but they may not have the knowledge or understanding of local politics to translate those general preferences into specific choices. It is precisely the voters who follow local affairs more closely who can determine whether a political challenger may provide better leadership than an incumbent. As we'll see in later chapters, these voters are far more likely to base their votes on specific issues and policies than on vague heuristics like partisanship or candidate charisma.

The third reason why low turnout may not be as problematic as we suppose is that voting is a very imprecise mechanism for expressing citizen preferences. Partly this is due to the nature of the ballot choices: not only are many local elections uncontested, but also the policy differences between candidates may not always represent existing cleavages in public opinion. In fact, for most candidates, the rational strategy in an election is to obfuscate one's position enough to appeal to the maximum number of voters (Tomz and Van Houweling 2009). Writing letters, making campaign contributions, speaking up in public meetings, and filing petitions are much more efficient mechanisms for conveying specific preferences.

This leads us to the biggest concern for the normative democratic theorist about low voter turnout: do homeowners and the educated, who are more likely to vote, have different political preferences than the less educated and renters? Many would say yes, and it is often argued that local politics is biased in favor of moneyed classes because property owners have a measurable financial interest in the decisions of their town (Logan and Molotch 1987). For example, zoning ordinances, street placement, utility services, and the construction of commercial areas can have a very large impact on property values and those with property have a very strong incentive to use local government to enhance the value of their investments.

While property development is a major political issue in many localities, there is nothing in the data presented in this chapter to suggest that the disproportionate turnout of homeowners and the educated is systematically distorting the tenor of local politics. It is difficult to identify any overarching set of political preferences that systematically divide voters and nonvoters in local elections. Although homeowners tend to be more politically informed and fiscally conservative than renters, these differences exist among both regular voters and nonregular voters; or rather, nonvoting homeowners are also more fiscally conservative than nonvoting renters. Because homeowners outnumber renters in most American localities, increasing local turnout is not likely to tip the overall balance of political preferences articulated through the ballot, especially because renters tend to have less clear preferences to begin with. In other words, the findings in this chapter suggest that even if all citizens were voting, the divisions in their policy preferences would largely remain.

This is not to imply that low turnout will always generate a representative outcome. In any place or instance where a governmental bias may serve some key constituent interests over others, the representativeness of lower turnout will become more questionable. Examples could include property developers who are seeking tax incentives or zoning easements, political organizations that seek to reward supporters with jobs or contracts, specific groups that might want a park in their neighborhood or sidewalks on their street. At some point in time, nearly every municipality is likely to encounter some type of issue that pits one group of citizens against another, or an instance where a minority interest is likely to benefit at the expense of a majority. In these cases, low turnout in a decisive election may lead to an undemocratic result. But such examples are more the exception than the rule in local democracy. For the overwhelming majority of local elections, a low turnout by an engaged and informed segment of the citizenry is sufficient for providing a representative basis for government.

CHAPTER 3

Who Runs for Local Office?

AS A STUDY IN CONTRASTS, it would be hard to find two politicians more dissimilar in personal and political style than Zenovia Evans and Jefferson "Zuma Jay" Wagner. Evans is an African American woman and the former mayor of Riverdale, Illinois, a working-class suburb on Chicago's south side. In public, she carries herself with a serious demeanor, talking in a straightforward manner with little sarcasm or humor. She is fervently pro-growth and spent much of her political career trying to lure investment and development into her economically struggling community. Wagner, by contrast, is the epitome of southern California mellow. An irreverent and jocular city council member in affluent Malibu, California, Wagner was best known among locals as the owner of a popular surf shop and for being an explosives expert in Hollywood. His central interest in local politics was to limit growth and development in Malibu, particularly in regard to commercial real estate and new housing.

Given these differences, one might expect both Evans and Wagner to have radically different ideas about politics and governing. Yet, politically speaking, they are cut from the same cloth. They are both long-term residents of their communities who were engaged in various civic projects before running for public office. They are property holders who are deeply attached to the towns in which they live. And, most importantly, both share a strong sense of civic obligation to do something to improve the quality of their communities.

The examples of Evans and Wagner highlight a puzzle when it comes to explaining local elections: can we understand what drives vote choice based on the types of candidates who are running?

This question is central to any issue regarding local politics. After all, *how* people vote largely depends on *who* they are voting for. The people who seek public office and the subsequent campaigns that they run fundamentally define the choices that voters face. If office seekers represent only a particular group, or if elections are dominated by one party (as in totalitarian states like Cuba and North Korea), then the very democratic character of the organization is questionable. In other words, who runs for office (and how they run) determines whether a democratic organization operates as a true democracy or a plutocracy, oligarchy, or de facto autocracy.

Characterizing candidates for local elections, however, is no easy task. During the past five decades, scholars and political observers have offered radically different perspectives on the types of people who run for and control city government. Some view municipal offices as the fiefdoms of local economic and social elites (Mills 1956; Hunter 1952); others see local government as captured by professional groups primarily concerned with real estate and growth (Logan and Molotch 1987); others characterize office seekers as party hacks, ideological zealots, or civically minded volunteers (Ehrenhalt 1992; Dahl 1961; Wolfinger 1974). The ethnographic research into this book only confirmed this pluralism of explanations. Every candidate interviewed not only had a distinct story and background but also a seemingly unique set of circumstances that lead him or her into public life. Some were driven by personal ambition, others by a sense of civic duty, others by appeals from friends or neighbors, and still others were motivated by particular issues. This variety creates a difficult challenge to understanding small-scale elections: how can we generalize about who runs for local office when the candidates seem so idiosyncratic? In other words, how do we compare a politician like John McCain or Barack Obama with one like Zenovia Evans or Jefferson "Zuma Jay" Wagner?

As with any aspect of small-scale elections, the answers to these questions hinge on the type of democratic organization in question. In other words, the types of people who run for office depend on the type of offices they are running for. A governorship attracts a different type of candidate and requires a different type of campaign than does a board seat on a mosquito abatement district or the treasurer of the local garden club. It is unlikely that a highly ambitious politico will run for a minor post because it affords neither power nor opportunity for higher office; conversely, someone motivated purely by civic duty is less likely to endure the time, effort, and expense necessary to run for a larger and more politically contentious post such as mayor, governor, or the head of a union. The first step, therefore, in understanding "who runs?" is to differentiate the *types of democracies* they are contesting. And to do this we can return to the theoretical framework outlined in chapter 1. Just as the size, scope, and bias of a democracy influences the types of people who vote, it also influences the types of people who run for office and the types of campaigns they run. In other words, the relative influence of personal ambition, civic responsibility, mobilizing issues, personal gain, political indignation or any other factor will vary according to where the democracy sits on these three scales.

This chapter examines the impact of these factors by looking at a large sample of local politicians (i.e., unsuccessful candidates and elected officials) from the greater Chicago metropolitan area. The small size, limited scope, and low bias of most Chicago-area municipal governments mean that these local politicians, like local voters, tend to be stakeholders in their communities. They are very concerned with issues of economic development and quality of life, yet are drawn into public affairs primarily from a sense of civic duty and an attachment to their towns. As in any managerial democracy, they are motivated less by ideology, partisanship, or even personal ambition, than by a public-spirited commitment to sustaining the quality of their communities. Like Evans and Wagner they may seem quite different to the naked eye, but beneath these outward traits are a host of similar characteristics that tend to define the local politician and coincide with the managerial character of local democracy.

WHO RUNS FOR LOCAL OFFICE?

> "You want to know what politics is? I'll tell you what it is. It's when you get a phone call at 12:30 in the night and one of your constituents calls up and says 'you get your ass over here and move this dog shit off my lawn.'"
>
> —Wilma Goldstein, *Vote for Me: Politics in America*

For all its putative glamour and prestige, holding elected office is typically hard and thankless work. No matter what the office, it usually involves a wide range of demanding and often tedious tasks: fundraising, networking, tending to constituents, long meetings, speechmaking, and maintaining public decorum. In common parlance, these are also known respectively as begging, schmoozing, babysitting, enduring, sweet-talking, and otherwise suffering fools gladly. And, for most locally elected offices in the United States, this is done for little or no pay. Given the significant costs and numerous indignities associated with nearly any elected office, why on earth would anyone seek to run at all?

This question is important to consider because the types of people who run for office are likely to influence the types of decisions that local governments make. Partly this is a matter of descriptive representation. If the only people who seek office are white, Protestant males, as with the American presidency until the 1920s, then other groups, such as women, nonwhites, or atheists, may be less likely to have their interests represented. Partly this is a matter of economic interest. If candidates come only from a certain social class or set of professions, then the concerns of those groups or their political agendas are likely to be prioritized. And partly this is a matter of democratic responsibility. If candidates are running only to enrich themselves or certain groups, then they are likely to govern and campaign through patronage or other mechanisms of corruption. Even personal qualities like ambition have a larger impact on democratic governance. Political theorists since James Madison have recognized that personal ambition can be utilized to sustain the responsiveness of democratic institutions: as elected officials continually seek to either maintain their current office or seek higher office, they are compelled to act in the public interest. Like the question of "Who votes?" in chapter 2, the question of "Who runs?" is essentially one about democratic accountability and performance.

So who runs in local elections? This is a complex question with no simple answer. Historians, biographers, social scientists, and political theorists have offered a seemingly endless array of explanations for why people choose to run for leadership posts, ranging from neo-Marxist theories about class structures to Freudian speculations about unconscious neuroses to more mundane (and practical) considerations such as the perceived quality of one's opponent. Most of these explanations are not mutually exclusive, and the one chosen usually depends on the orientation of the researcher. Biographers and historians are more likely to focus on individual personality traits while social scientists often seek answers in more quantifiable or largely social terms. But because most of these explanations tend to focus on larger historical figures holding powerful offices, the cumulative suitability of such accounts for small-scale democracies is unclear. In other words, a lot of ink has been spilled on most presidents and some particularly notable big-city mayors or congressional members; almost no biographies have been written on city council members, clerks, or board members of water management districts. Consequently, to figure out who runs for local office, we need to focus on the explanations that are most likely to be salient. These, it turns out, are quite similar to the factors that inspire people to vote: intrinsic motivations, extrinsic motivations, and opportunities.

Intrinsic motivations are the psychological rewards that one gets from running for and holding office. These motivations are particular to each individual and can take any number for forms. Examples can include feelings of self-fulfillment or aggrandizement; a sense of civic duty or obligation to one's community or organization; a feeling of outrage or indignation from a perceived slight or injustice from a certain party or current officeholder; an inexorable drive to take control over any kind of situation, particularly ones that are in crisis or disrepair; or a need to compensate for a feeling of inadequacy or insecurity relative to one's peers. What all of these examples of intrinsic motivations share is that they are largely intangible, difficult for outsiders to measure, and subjectively experienced. Politics for intrinsically motivated candidates is an end in itself, a life activity that confers its own rewards. Although all of these intrinsic motivations will be evident in any candidate (one has to like politics to run for office), for the purposes of this study we shall focus on one motivation in particular: feelings of civic duty.

Extrinsic motivations relate to the tangible social or material benefits from holding office. Although extrinsic rewards are partially subjective in nature (i.e., "one person's trash is another one's treasure"), they are, nevertheless, typically material and visible to an outside observer. Such rewards may involve particular benefits to the officeholder such as power, money, or outward self-aggrandizement, but they may also include fulfillment of desires to enact certain policies, to realize larger ideological goals. Examples of extrinsically motivated candidates include those who enriched themselves through their office, such as the notorious George Washington Plunkett of the Tammany Hall machine in New York (famous for saying "I seen my opportunities and I took 'em."); politicians obsessed with amassing power, like Lyndon Johnson; or ideologues like a Sarah Palin or Ralph Nader. They may be driven by a particular issue agenda, as with a member of the Green Party or an antiabortion activist. For the extrinsically motivated, politics is a means toward some other end, a vehicle that is useful for them to achieve some other goal. Here, we will focus on the three most common extrinsic motivations in politics: ideology, personal advancement, and material rewards for particular groups.

The last category of explanation for "Who runs?" is circumstance. This category is more amorphous because a wide variety of elements fall under its heading. Circumstance may refer to a particular opportunity as when a scandal, death, or administrative appointment suddenly creates a new opening—success in politics, after all, is often attributable to being at the right place at the right time. Circumstance may also be a function of social position. Who one knows and socializes with may be crucial to whether one is inspired or recruited to seek an office. For instance, many municipal officeholders get started in public life by serving on town planning boards, the bodies that approve construction permits and review zoning procedures. These boards often have vacancies, but the existing members of the boards and elected officials also have strong incentives to seek candidates who are not only knowledgeable about development matters but who will also be easy to work with. Such people are thus likely to draw on professional and social contacts and will prioritize people they know. Finally, circumstance may depend on a particular event that irks or inspires an otherwise docile citizen to take charge and seek office. For example, many candidates for suburban office get involved in objection to various land developments that threaten the status quo of their communities.

All three of these factors (intrinsic motivations, extrinsic motivations, and opportunity) are likely to be evident in any candidate's decision to run, but some are more likely to influence seekers of certain offices than others: the vice-presidency of a garden club is unlikely to offer many opportunities for corruption or to advance an ideological agenda, whereas a seat on the Chicago city council historically has generated many opportunities for personal enrichment. Thus the task in explaining "Who runs?" is to identify when these different types of motivations or opportunities are likely to be most salient. In other words, which offices attract the ambitious, the idealistic, the corrupt, the socially well-connected, and the opportunistic? The answer to this question can be found partly in the size, scope, and bias of the democratic organization in question.

Think about what a democracy's size means for any potential candidate. Larger democracies have bigger budgets, grander projects, higher capital campaigns, and, quite simply, more impact on the world around them. Larger democracies also present greater challenges for anyone seeking office—not only do they usually encompass greater internal diversity, but they also are more likely to entertain conflicts in regard to their larger projects. For example, Michael Bloomberg, the current mayor of New York, has responsibilities that are not dissimilar to that of a governor of a large state, whereas Gerald Daus, the village president of Golf, Illinois, has far fewer tasks demanding his attention. Furthermore, running for office in a larger democracy will also be more taxing than in a smaller place if for no other reason than it simply requires attracting more votes. Whereas Daus probably knows everyone who might vote in his village, Bloomberg could only personally know, much less meet, a miniscule fraction of his constituents. Running for office in a larger democracy will thus require more resources and a much greater campaign effort.

A democracy's scope will also influence the types of people who run. Democracies that are limited in scope, such as a mosquito abatement district or a garden club, are unlikely to attract candidates who are motivated by grandiose personal ambitions, strong ideological goals, or other any other extrinsic motivations, because their institutional powers are so circumscribed; if a democracy's missions and bylaws strictly limit the range of its activities, then its leaders will have few opportunities to advance any particular beliefs or even to promote their own accomplishments. For such narrow-scope democracies, it is more likely that candidates are motivated by intrinsic factors such as a sense of civic duty, social obligation, or peer pressure. Their willingness to serve in a leadership role will reflect a sense of personal responsibility and also be a function of circumstance, particularly if they were recruited to serve.

However, as the scope of a democracy grows, it is more likely to attract extrinsically motivated candidates. This can be illustrated by comparing a mosquito abatement district board member with a county supervisor. In most states, counties have a broad range of powers from policing to land usage, and their ability to exercise or expand those powers is often dependent on the initiative of individual members. A county office is thus more likely to attract candidates who have more well-formed ideas about the role of the state in society; conservatives may seek to use county offices to promote economic development or, at the least, limit regulation on local business, while liberals may seek to expand government services to redress social inequities. None of these powers is likely to be evident in a mosquito abatement board—it is hard to imagine how a conservative vision of mosquito eradication would substantially differ from a liberal one (although a Green Party candidate may have some distinct opinions from the two). Similarly, the broader powers of a county board member give greater opportunity for building a network of donors, political contacts, and party links that can provide an excellent springboard for higher office.

Finally, the types of people who run for office will be influenced by a democracy's bias (i.e., how skewed it distributes its services, resources, etc.). If a democracy is universalistic in its allocation of resources, then candidates will have few motivations to mobilize particular constituencies. For a candidate running for mayor of an affluent suburb like Glencoe, Illinois, it makes little sense to target just some residents, because they all get roughly equivalent levels of police and fire protection, library privileges, and other municipal services simply from living in the town. However, when a democracy differentiates its services or redistributes goods to a particular group, it creates a strong motivation for candidates who either are primarily concerned with the well-being of the subgroup receiving benefits, or are seeking to personally enrich themselves through graft and kickbacks from the privileged groups. In other words, it draws in extrinsically motivated candidates.

The iconic example of a candidate in a biased democracy is the machine politician. Throughout most of their history, America's larger, older cities have had political machines—partisan organizations that sought to acquire office and control public resources to further the material ends of the organizational leaders. Machine candidates are either at the top of the machine (such as a mayor or governor) or intermediary officers (as with city council candidates who are also ward bosses). Bias in a democracy, however, may not always contribute to graft and corruption: some candidates may be motivated simply to protect what they view as a just or proper redistribution of a democracy's resources. An example of this may be an idealistic candidate who seeks to increase social services to the poor and indigent or a candidate from the business community who wants government to spend more on services that promote economic development.

The size, scope, and bias of a democracy will shape not only the types of people who run for office, but also the types of campaigns they are likely to run for. Intrinsically motivated candidates are less likely to invest a lot of their own resources or spend a lot of time fundraising, because the rewards of their office are so much less significant. If I am running for treasurer of the garden club, a board member on the mosquito abatement district, or any other office that has little power and offers no pay, I am unlikely to extend myself to further meet an already burdensome civic obligation. As the size of a democracy increases and as the extrinsic rewards of office begin to grow, however, candidates will be far more likely to engage in professional campaigning. This will include raising money, running advertisements, mobilizing supporters, and trying to charm constituents.

Scope and bias will also shape campaign activities. Democracies that are broad in scope are more likely to attract ideological candidates who will utilize, in turn, more ideological appeals to their constituents. For instance, candidates for congress, governorships, and the presidency nearly always utilize lists from either conservative or liberal organizations as a mechanism for fundraising and mobilizing supporters. Similarly, biased democracies would see candidates using material incentives to mobilize the key constituents that are disproportionately benefiting. Once again, the classic examples of this are the jobs, services, and perks that political machines offer to voters in exchange for their support on election day.

To summarize, the types of people who seek office and the campaigns they run are relative to the size, scope, and bias of a democracy. When a democracy is small, limited in scope, and nonbiased in the distribution of resources, the motivations for seeking public office will typically be those of civic duty, responsibility, or social obligation. Although the occasional issue or particular event may motivate a run for office, most candidates are driven by concerns that are neither ideological nor materially self-serving. In such organizations, one should find limited campaigning and low-visibility elections. However, as the size, scope, and/or bias of a democracy grow, candidate motivations will become more extrinsic. Ambitious and ideological candidates will campaign harder, seek to mobilize core constituencies, employ ideological or issue-based appeals, and will govern in a more particularistic fashion. To better understand this point, let us turn our attention to some data on actual politicians.

WHO RUNS FOR LOCAL OFFICE?

In the universe of democratic organizations, most municipalities are smaller, limited in scope, and less biased in the distribution of their services. As noted in previous chapters, most American municipalities are under 5,000 in population, are limited in their discretionary power, and allocate most of their budgets on universalistic programs such as police and fire protection, street maintenance, libraries, and administrative services. Consequently, it is unlikely they will attract candidates who are going to be motivated by political ambitions for higher office, by dreams of personal financial aggrandizement, or by burning ideological goals. Rather, candidates should be distinguished more by their interests in their communities, their sense of civic duty, and the social connections that link them to fellow citizens.

Looking at actual candidates for a sample of Illinois municipal offices, this supposition about the intrinsic motivation of local politicians seems borne out. In 2008, mayors, city council members and unsuccessful candidates for these offices were surveyed in three Chicago-area counties: Cook, Lake, and DuPage.[1] The survey sampled from a wide variety of places in terms of population size, income, and racial composition, although most Chicago-area municipalities, like suburbs across the country, were predominantly white, middle-class, and between 2,500 and 50,000 in population.[2]

---

[1] An initial mail survey was sent to a list of 700 current officeholders in the summer of 2008. These office holders were randomly picked from a list of all mayors and council members in the three counties. Of the original 700 surveys sent out, a total of 354 completed surveys were returned either by mail or through follow-up phone calls. In order to compare differences between winners and losers in local elections, an additional phone survey was conducted between September 2008 and February 2009 of candidates who had run for local office but had not been elected in 2007. Non-winning candidates were contacted who had received at least 10 percent of the vote and who had a publicly listed phone number. An attempted contact was made for all of the candidates who met these criteria with fifty-eight candidates actually being interviewed. Seventy-nine percent of the sample was either a candidate or a currently-serving council member; 21 percent were candidates or currently-serving mayors.

[2] A majority of respondents (55 percent) came from middle-sized municipalities (i.e., between 10,000 and 50,000 in population), 32 percent came from small places (i.e., place under 10,000 in population), and 13 percent were from large suburbs (over 50,000 in population). The sample spans a broad range of income categories as well: 11 percent

Thus, while this survey is not representative of local candidates across the country as a whole (because it does not draw upon a national sample), the types of communities it encompasses are not very far in composition from municipalities in general.[3] With these grains of salt in mind, the results from this survey are unlikely to be very dissimilar from results that would be found in any sample of smaller American municipalities.

Starting with some simple demographic statistics about people who hold and run for local office (see table 3.1), one is immediately struck by the particularities of these local politicians. The overwhelming majority are white, college-educated, male, older, homeowners, and do not fit the profile of someone who would run for office for either personal aggrandizement or career advancement. Consider, for instance, the simple fact that local candidates are, on average, much older than the general population: half are between the ages of 50 and 64, and one in five is a senior citizen. Indeed, only 5 percent of the sample is under 40. Simply by their age alone, it is unlikely that these are a group looking to use local politics as a vehicle for a further career (although more on this later).

Socioeconomic status is also found to have an important relationship to civic duty among local office-seekers. Compared to the general population, suburban officeholders and candidates are much more educated and more likely to be in professional careers. For instance, nearly three-quarters of the sample have a college degree and over one-third have some kind of graduate degree as well. They are almost all homeowners (99.5 percent), and most have been long-term residents of their communities, with over 75 percent of respondents having reported living in their communities

---

were from places with a median household income under $45,000 a year; 48 percent were from places with a median household income between $45,000 and $66,000; 28 percent were from places with a median household income between $66,000 and $99,000; and, 13 percent were from places with a median household income above $99,000 a year. Just over 12 percent of the sample were from majority nonwhite municipalities and 22 percent were predominantly white places (i.e., over 90 percent white), while 48 percent of the sample came from places between 70 and 90 percent white.

[3] The sample is notable for its whiteness: nearly 9 in 10 suburban elected officials or candidates are white; only 6 percent are black and 3 percent are Latino. This is consistent with the overrepresentation of whites in city council positions (Hajnal and Trounstine 2005).

TABLE 3.1
Demographic Characteristics of Chicago-Area Office Holders

	Percent		Percent
Age		*Education*	
Under 40	5	H.S. Degree or Less	11
40–49	22	Some College	18
50–64	52	College Degree	35
Over 64	21	Graduate Degree	36
Race		*Homeownership*	
White	89	Own Home	99.5
Black	6	Rent	.5
Latino	3		
Other	2	*Profession*	
		Management	28
Length of Residence		Lawyer	9
< 10 years	8	Real Estate	9
10 – 20 years	14	Self-Employed	9
> 20 years	78	Retired	13
		Public Sector	12
Sex		Banking	4
Male	74	Sales	5
Female	26	Other Professions	11

Source: Authors' 2008–2009 survey of Chicago-area politicians; ncases = 358.

for more than 20 years. Although the politicians surveyed hold a wide variety of occupations, the highest numbers are in management, public sector, law or other professions, like physicians and dentists. For example, 28 percent reported being in high-level management positions (i.e., supervisors, vice presidents, presidents) or holding a nonlegal professional degree. Lawyers and people working in real estate each made up 9 percent of the sample. About 9 percent of the sample was self-employed, 13 percent were retired, and 12 percent worked in the public sector. The other major occupational categories represented were banking (4 percent) and sales (5 percent). Ten percent had nonmanagement jobs or worked in trades.

Such occupations provide further evidence of civic voluntarism as a primary motivation for holding local elected office. Not only are local politicians older as a group, they are, on the whole, already engaged in full-time professional careers or are retired. For most of this group, the prestige of being a local council member or mayor is probably on par, if not below, the social status they already have in their careers. Furthermore, it is unlikely that these people have much extra time or energy to engage in a full-time political career. When asked about how much time they spend on local politics, roughly half the sample said 10 hours a week or less, and 80 percent reported working less than 20 hours a week. Only 5 percent of the sample reported working more than 40 hours a week on local affairs. For the overwhelming majority of local politicians, running for and holding office is a part-time activity.

The politicians were also asked directly if they "had any ambitions to run for higher office" and, if they said yes, which one they would pursue. Although nearly 30 percent of the sample indicated some ambition for higher office, the overwhelming majority of these (68 percent) were city council members who were interested in being mayor or village president, and about 27 percent indicated interest in running for the state legislature or for a county board position. Interestingly though, many candidates acknowledged that their chances of achieving these offices depended on circumstances beyond their control (such as the current mayor stepping down) or were probably out of reach (for reasons of gerrymandering in state legislative districts among others). Even given these nods to ambition, we could still characterize most local politicians as part-time politicos with modest political career goals.

If local politicians are not primarily driven by ambition for personal advancement, then perhaps they are driven by the concerns of their local economic milieu, in particular that of a property-developing "growth machine." Here the evidence is somewhat stronger, although the characterization of local politics as being dominated by property valuation appears to be an overstatement. Consider, once again, the career choices of our sample of local politicians. Obviously, a significant number come from industries related to property development such as real estate, law, insurance, and banking. But while such careers are overrepresented, they do not entirely dominate the local political classes. In fact, they are not even a plurality of local politicians. Rather, a majority come from professions that have little to do with real estate: the self-employed, doctors, teachers, business managers, sales, firemen, and other jobs in the public sector. Given this diversity of professional backgrounds, a more accurate characterization of these local officeholders is not that they are property mavens but, instead, stakeholders. Like the citizens who frequently vote in local elections (see chapter 2), the candidates who run in local elections are nearly all homeowners and long-term residents of their communities. They are people who seem to have an intrinsic liking of politics and feel strongly about the well-being of their communities.

This civic orientation is clearly evident in their self-expressed motivations for holding public office. The local politicians were asked an open-ended question about what initially motivated them to run for local office. The categorized results are listed in figure 3.1. Nearly half of the respondents reported running either because of a sense of civic duty *or* because they first worked in an affiliated community organization. One of the most common explanations was that they "owed something to the community" or that it "was a civic obligation." Although the self-serving nature of such responses may elicit some skepticism, this was an anonymous survey and respondents had little reason to promote their own self-image. In one-on-one interviews, most politicians appeared sincere about their deep interest in their towns. Many of these officials got their start by beginning work with an affiliated civic organization, such as a zoning board, park and recreation board, or PTA. And, as a pathway to local politics, this makes sense. After all, people who are willing to serve on a zoning board or president of their local Little League are the types of people willing to get involved in larger community issues.

Beyond a sense of civic duty, the second most popular pathway to local politics was being recruited by someone else. In fact, nearly a quarter of the sample said they held their current position because they were appointed by a mayor, were recruited by another politician, or were drawn into politics by an active family mem-

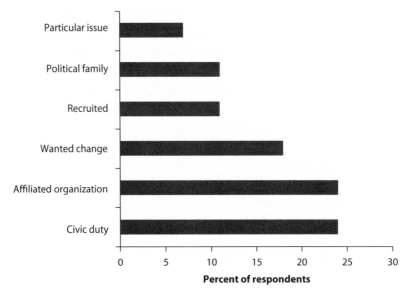

Figure 3.1. Motivations for running for public office. *Source*: Authors' 2008–2009 survey of Chicago-area politicians (ncases = 358).

ber. Many of these made themselves available for recruitment by working on community boards or through social ties from family members who were active in politics. As in national politics, who you know seems to be a crucial factor for determining whether someone gets involved in local affairs.

Interestingly, the least common pathway to local politics was a particular issue. Fewer than 10 percent of the sample indicated a particular problem or concern that motivated their involvement. When asked to specify that concern, most of them indicated, not surprisingly, issues regarding property development or taxation. A number said they were motivated by "disappointment with incumbents' performance" or they wanted to make their community "more competitive" or had other concerns about "the direction" of their towns. Several indicated concerns with fiscal management of their communities and "thought they could do better" than the current leadership. Several, for example, mentioned particular development plans that they objected to, while others often cited fiscal concerns or other issues regarding how town funds were spent. Yet, the number of these issue-motivated politicians was dwarfed by the larger number who mentioned either civic duty or simply being recruited. From this sample, local politicians seem primarily motivated by their concerns with community and by social networks than anything else.

Such strong civic mindedness, however, does not mean they are innocent of ideology or partisan politics. Local politicians are, after all, people willing to spend much of their free time in public affairs and, like any big consumers of political information, they tend to have highly developed ideas about the role of the state in society and tend to be affiliated with larger political organizations. Interestingly though, despite being political elites, their ideology and partisanship is often unrelated to their local political service. This stands in sharp contrast with holders of large-scale offices. Indeed, nearly every member of Congress and state legislator belongs to a political party and most have very well-defined political ideologies that are either to the right or left of the average American (McCarty, Poole, and Rosenthal 2006). This is not the case in among the local politicians surveyed. Although they were more likely to identify as Republican and as ideologically conservative, a large number did not formally identify with any political party or with either end of the political spectrum. Specifically, 43 percent of the sample identified themselves as Republicans, 25 percent as Democrats, and 32 percent as independents or affiliated with a third party (see figure 3.2). Compared to the public at large, this is a disproportionately high number of Republicans; compared to most elected officials, this is a very high percentage of independents. This last fact is very curious because in national surveys, the overwhelming majority of Americans who are very interested in local politics also affiliate themselves with a political party (Lewis-Beck et al. 2008). The high number of independents in this sample is likely due to the large number of nonpartisan elections in the Chicago area. In other words, these independents are people who probably vote very regularly with the parties in state and national elections but genuinely consider themselves independent when it comes to local affairs.

Another reason for the high number of independents among the survey respondents may have to do with ideology. A majority of

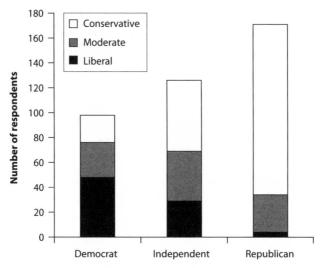

Figure 3.2. Partisanship and ideology among Chicago-area elected officials. *Source*: Authors' 2008–2009 survey of Chicago-area politicians (ncases = 358).

the sample (54 percent) identify themselves as conservative, 25 percent identify as moderate, and 21 percent call themselves liberal. This ideological breakdown corresponds with their party identification: 80 percent of Republicans also identified as conservative, compared to only 50 percent of independents and 21 percent of Democrats. Conversely, Democrats were far more likely to identify as liberals (50 percent), with a third calling themselves moderates and 21 percent as conservative. Independents divided themselves almost evenly between conservative and either liberal or moderate. Given the high number of conservatives and moderates calling themselves "independents," it is also possible that many in this group may be ideologically disaffected Republicans or are shifting to be more in line with their constituents. As in many northern American metropolitan areas, Chicago's suburbs have been trending more Democratic in their voting in recent presidential and congressional elections, and such trends may be evident in these patterns of partisanship among the elected officials.

The relatively high level of nonpartisanship and ideological moderation of the survey respondents may also reflect the lack of political conflict in the communities they represent. In the survey, the local politicians were asked to evaluate the level of personal conflict and ideological division within their towns.[4] On the whole, there seems to be little political or ideological conflict in most of Chicago's suburbs. Only 10 percent of respondents reported sharp ideological divisions within their communities, and only 20 percent thought that local politics were highly personalized in their conflicts. A majority rated only moderate ideological divisions where they live, and roughly a third of respondents reported very little conflict or division. It is worth noting that these two indicators are highly correlated with one another: in other words, respondents in places with high levels of ideological conflict were also more likely to report high levels of personal conflict in local politics as well. Although the municipalities may not be uniformly tranquil, the tone of politics in most places appears civil and the divisions among residents not tremendous.

This is not to suggest, however, that local political life is without any important issues. In the survey, the Chicago-area politicians were given a list of twelve items common in local politics and asked them to identify all of the ones that they thought were important in the previous election. Figure 3.3 depicts the percent of respondents marking issues from the twelve different categories. Not surprisingly, local politics seems primarily concerned with issues of economic and property development; cumulatively, over 80 percent of local politicians indicated that at least one of these two issues was important in the previous campaign. Local politics is primarily about land and money, as previous scholars have noted, and this continues to be evident in the campaign issues. In follow-up conversations with a subsample of the Chicago-area politicians, they almost all expressed concern about the economic well-being of their communities. This usually included the state of commercial business districts or proposals to expand property developments,

---

[4] The survey asked "In some towns, local politics involves a lot of personal conflicts while in others, politics remains cordial and professional. How about in your town? Using the 10 point scale below, how would you rate the tenor of local politics in your community?" and "In some towns, most citizens have the same ideology or political views, while in other places, citizens are very divided along political lines. What about in your town? Using this 10 point scale, could you indicate the level of political division in your town?"

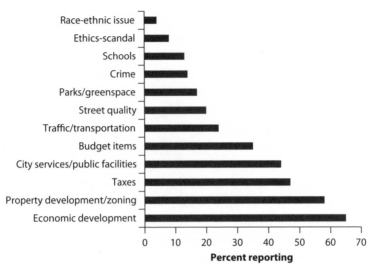

Figure 3.3. Most common campaign issues in suburban elections. *Source*: Authors' 2008–2009 survey of Chicago-area politicians (ncases = 358).

although the nature of these debates tended to vary from place to place. In some communities, the primary concern was with re- stricting growth and keeping the status quo, while in other places, the emphasis was on drawing in more employers and expanding the retail base of the community. As will be detailed below, much of this depended on the economic status of the suburb: affluent places tended to resist further development while poorer suburbs often sought to bring it in.

The second most important issue concerned the administration of public services. This included concerns over taxes, budget spend- ing, and the quality of municipal services. Nearly half the respon- dents indicated that taxes were a campaign issue, and 45 percent listed a specific type of city service as having come under scrutiny. About a third of the politicians indicated debate over a budget item, usually based on controversy over some spending plan. Few people like to pay taxes, and nearly all the politicians interviewed indicated a strong voter sentiment to keep them lower. Neverthe- less, voters also want particular services, and these demands put local politicians in the difficult position of trying to restrain the budget while keeping, or sometimes expanding, their municipalities' programs. Beyond these issues, concerns with traffic congestion, parks and "green space" preservation, and, yes potholes, each were indicated by about 20 percent of the politicians.

Interestingly, most of the issues that preoccupy voters in big-city elections were not very evident in the survey; fewer than 20 percent of local politicians indicated that crime or schools were important in their local campaigns. These low numbers may not only reflect a lower crime rate in many of their suburbs but the fact that schools are often administered by independent school districts and were not the responsibility of the local municipality. At the bottom of the list were issues pertaining to race or the presence of any scandals. Once again, given the racial homogeneity of most suburbs and the limited opportunities for personal malfeasance, many of the staples of politics in nearby Chicago are simply not issues in its neighboring suburbs.

Taking all of these findings together, an ironic picture of local politicians begins to emerge. These are leaders who must confront important issues facing their communities and differentiate themselves from their competitors on these issues, but the issues themselves are not what usually motivate them to run for office. And while they are not innocent of ideology or partisan politics (these are, after all, people who are willing to spend much of their free time in public affairs), such factors are not what bring them into local political life. Instead, the overwhelming majority are motivated by a profound sense of civic duty. Although some have ambition and some are ideological, these concerns more often are subsumed by a much greater force: a strong interest in the affairs of their community. In short, local politicians are not just stakeholders, but stakeholders with a strong sense of social obligation or a need to take charge.

How Do Local Politicians Run Their Campaigns?

Among political professionals there is a well-established, conventional wisdom about how to run a local campaign: ingratiate yourself to local party leaders, make yourself known to local organizations; raise a lot of money; build a political "team"; canvas voters by knocking on doors; send out fliers, press releases, and other "professional" materials; and, seemingly most important, blanket your constituency with ubiquitous yard signs displaying your name. While undoubtedly all of this advice makes good sense, there is very little systematic evidence showing what, if any, decisive difference such activities make. And while proof about the efficacy of such efforts awaits experimentation, we can in the meantime, examine what types of campaign activities suburban politicians do engage in and how these vary according to the type of community they are running in.

Returning to the Chicago-area survey data, table 3.2 lists the percentage of local politicians who engaged in various campaign activities by the office they were seeking (mayor versus council) and whether they won or lost the last election. Activities included whether they held office before, got newspaper endorsements, received support from their local party (usually the county organization), spent a certain amount on their campaign, and engaged in different types of advertising and mobilization efforts. The table also indicates the percent of voters the candidates estimated that they personally knew.

Although there are some notable differences in the campaigns (particularly between mayors and council members), what is far more striking is the overall similarities in campaign activities. Let us start with the few differences. The biggest was the political experience between mayors and council members. Roughly 8 in 10 mayoral candidates (both winners and losers) had previous experience in office and the most common experience among these mayors was being a city council member. By contrast, the least experienced group tended to be current city council members. Fewer than one in four had previously held elected office, a number that was even lower than unsuccessful candidates for city council positions. The lower level of experience among successful city council experience reflects the fact that many had uncontested elections or were appointed to their positions.

Another difference between winners and losers of local elections appears to be in the level of outside support and endorse-

TABLE 3.2
Campaign Activities by Office Sought

	Mayor (won)	Mayor (lost)	Council (won)	Council (lost)
Previous Experience	88	84	23	36
Newspaper Endorsed	64	42	36	56
Opponent Endorsed by Paper	26	62	35	48
Support from Local Party	22	11	16	16
Spent under $5,000*	37	47	69	69
Spent over $7,500*	57	32	23	17
Campaigning: Yard Signs*	94	88	87	88
Campaigning: Mailings*	95	65	74	67
Campaigning: Fliers*	74	88	72	67
Mobilized Voters (Phone)*	60	53	44	38
Mobilized Voters (Door)*	86	100	82	92
Mobilized Voters (email)*	32	41	33	29
Ncases	70	16	284	42

Source: Authors' 2008–2009 survey of Chicago-area politicians; ncases = 358.
Note: Numbers in the table are percentages.
*contested races

ments. About two-thirds of the winning mayoral candidates were endorsed by a local paper compared to only 40 percent of their unsuccessful counterparts. Winning mayoral candidates were twice as likely to have received some support from a local party organization, although this overall number was quite small (about one five). Among council candidates, the differences between winners and losers and the overall rates of newspaper endorsements and party support were much lower. In fact, newspaper endorsements and party support seemed to have little bearing on winning city council races: a majority of unsuccessful council candidates reported having a newspaper endorsement, compared to roughly a third of successful ones. Once again, this last figure may be misleading, however, because a significant portion (22 percent) of winning city council members ran unopposed, which might have precluded endorsements.

Campaign spending also seems to differentiate winning and losing mayoral candidates but, once again, money appears to be less important for city council races. Looking only at contested races, 57 percent of winning mayoral candidates spent over $7,500 on their campaign compared to only 32 percent of non-winning candidates. The overwhelming majority of council candidates (69 percent) spent under $5,000 on their campaigns, although winning candidates were more likely to have spent over $7,500 on their campaigns. Although not listed in the table, there was also a big difference between mayors and council candidates in very high levels of campaign spending. Over 40 percent of mayoral candidates reported spending more than $10,000 on their campaigns compared to less than 12 percent of council candidates.

In terms of campaign activities, there are only a few notable differences among the four categories of candidates. Printing and posting yard signs was nearly universal among all categories of candidates as was canvassing voters door to door: roughly nine in ten candidates did both of these activities. Beyond these similarities there were some slight differences. Winning mayoral and council candidates were slightly more likely to use mailings although non-winning mayor candidates were more likely to use fliers (which may reflect differences in their campaign budgets, with mailings being more expensive than fliers). Winning candidates were slightly more likely to have mobilized voters by phone, although a higher percentage of non-winning mayoral candidates used email. By and large, however, these differences are rather minor and what is more remarkable is the high level of consistency among all kinds of candidates in their campaign activities. It appears that most candidates are getting their information about how to campaign from the same sources and generally follow similar strategies in getting elected.

Size, Scope, and Bias in Local Campaigns

Of course many of these differences may also be attributable to the types of communities where the candidates are running, and, as discussed earlier, we should expect to see differences in campaigning by their size, scope, and bias. Although Chicago-area suburbs are somewhat limited in their ranges on these scales as a whole (they tend to be smaller, limited in scope, and universalistic in their service provision), we do see some interesting differences in campaigning when comparing them across two of these three dimensions, namely population size and income. Table 3.3 lists the average spending patterns, campaign activities, and mobilization efforts for all candidates, broken down by the size and median household income of their municipality.

First, campaigning in a larger suburb is a more intense activity than campaigning in a smaller one. Politicians in larger places are more vigorous campaigners and spend more on their campaigns. For example, only 9 percent of the candidates in the smallest suburbs (places under 10,000 in population) spent more than $7,500 on their campaigns compared to 68 percent of those in places between 50,000 and 75,000 in population. Conversely, only about a quarter of candidates in the largest places spent less than $5,000 on their campaigns compared to about 80 percent of the candidates in the smallest places. Candidates in larger suburbs are also more likely to use mailings, yard signs, and fliers and are also more likely to mobilize voters over the phone. Interestingly, there are no differences in retail activities such as canvassing voters door-to-door—politicians all seem compelled to do this regardless of the size of their community.

These differences in campaign activities between large and small places are not surprising. As the number of potential voters increases, a campaigner must do more to reach them. This requires more mass-scale activities such as advertising and mass mailings. Such activities, of course, also require more money, which, in turn, requires a host of other campaign activities such as fundraising and recruiting more staff and volunteers. Quite simply, running for

TABLE 3.3
Campaign Activities by Place Size and Income Level

By Place Size	<10,000	10–25,000	25–50,000	50–75,000	>75,000
Spent under $5,000	82	68	63	30	22
Spent over $7,500	9	23	25	68	50
Campaigning: Yard Signs	80	84	88	95	94
Campaigning: Mailings	66	76	71	92	76
Campaigning: Fliers	68	70	76	92	65
Mobilized Voters (Phone)	39	47	49	59	35
Mobilized Voters (Door)	79	90	79	89	88
Mobilized Voters (Email)	17	40	36	43	35
By Median Income	< $45k	$45-58k	$58-66k	$66-99k	>$99k
Spent under $5,000	60	61	63	72	73
Spent over $7,500	24	29	27	21	18
Campaigning: Yard Signs	93	82	89	85	76
Campaigning: Mailings	69	78	77	68	74
Campaigning: Fliers	91	74	77	69	50
Mobilized Voters (Phone)	49	45	45	41	52
Mobilized Voters (Door)	91	86	93	86	50
Mobilized Voters (Email)	16	18	39	36	41

Source: Authors' 2008–2009 survey of Chicago-area politicians; ncases = 358.
Note: Numbers in the table are percentages

office in a larger place requires a much more serious investment of time and energy.

The other interesting differences in campaign activities are evident in the comparisons by the income of a community. As I described in chapter 1, income may inadvertently be an indicator of bias in a municipality, because the impact of government decisions are more financially meaningful in a poor community. In line with this hypothesis, we see a surprising pattern in campaign spending across different community income levels: candidates in wealthier suburbs tend to spend much less on their campaigns than candidates in poorer ones. For example, nearly a quarter of the candidates in suburbs with a median income below $45,000 a year spent over $7,500 on their campaign compared to only 18 percent of the candidates in the wealthiest suburbs (places with a median household income above $99,000). Meanwhile, nearly three-quarters of the candidates in the wealthiest suburbs spent the absolute lowest amounts on their campaigns compared to only 60 percent of those in the poorest places.

Now these trends are partly a function of population (the most affluent places tend to be under 10,000 in population), but they also reflect the more sedate nature of campaigning in wealthy suburbs. In the survey, the most affluent suburbs were more than twice as likely to have uncontested elections as the poorest ones, and also electioneering in such wealthy places tended to be far quieter affairs. For example, only half the candidates in the wealthiest places distributed campaign fliers compared to 91 percent of the candidates in the poorest places. Politicians in wealthier suburbs were also much less likely to use yard signs or knock on resident doors although, not surprisingly, they were more likely to mobilize supporters via email.

CONCLUSION

In examining "who runs" for local office, we come to a rather ironic conclusion. Local politics is dominated by a particular element of society, but its particularity is not defined necessarily by its economic or social preeminence as much as by its civic commitments. Local politicians tend to be older, more educated, and more professional than the general population, but it is not these characteristics that determine their trajectory toward political power. There are plenty of older, educated professionals who don't care a lick about local politics. Rather, local politicians are distinguished by their intense feelings of civic obligation and interest in the affairs of their communities. After all, few American suburbs lack a large number of educated and qualified citizens who could run for public office; what differentiates those who heed the call of local politics is their particular interest in local affairs. Holding office for them is generally not a springboard for higher office, a mechanism for personal enrichment, or a vehicle to exercise an ideological vision. Rather local politics is an activity with intrinsic rewards in itself.

The irony, though, is that for all their civic virtue, local politicians are still encountering meaningful and important issues in the course of their political lives. They make particular allocations of scarce resources, often choose between unpleasant alternatives of cutting services or raising taxes, and decide on issues that will not necessarily coincide with the preferences of all their neighbors. As we'll see throughout this book, most local politicians inevitably face important, substantive issues that often divide their constituencies. The fact that these issues are parochial and temporal makes them easy to overlook. But ask any local politician about spending hours confronting angry voters over a decision to build a public restroom or expand a parking lot, and they will testify to the passion locals often hold about these seemingly mundane questions. As a result, local politicians inevitably face some level of animus for sometimes the most mundane of decisions. Because of the relative costs of making these difficult issues compared to their paltry extrinsic rewards, local politicians would seem to exemplify the notion that "no good deed goes unpunished."

This picture of local politicians stands in sharp contrast to the scholarly assessments of local leadership. Ever since the 1950s, social scientists have focused on the elite status of leaders, typically in large cities. Not only do local politicians putatively arise from a community's economically dominant strata, they govern at the behest of vested commercial interests that are primarily focused with improving the market values of commercial properties. Where there are exceptions to this rule, they tend to be party bosses or ambitious politicians from ethnic groups who distribute political patronage as a mechanism for keeping power and advancing their own material interests (Wolfinger 1974).

Yet while these characterizations may have been appropriate to their place and time, they do not seem to hold for most American municipalities today. Nearly all of the case studies and research that support the models of the "machine boss," the "ethnic politician," or the "growth regime" are based on the study of just a handful of larger cities. America is no longer a country dominated by its large urban cores. Most Americans, even in metropolitan areas, live in communities that are much smaller in size, narrower in scope, and are less biased in the administration of their services. Few are sufficiently stratified along either racial or economic lines to generate a particular governing class whose economic interests stand in sharp contrast to the majority of residents. In most of these places, particularly among smaller places, there are few opportunities for massive commercial land speculation. Consequently, the driving forces identified by traditional models of urban politics simply are not germane to the vast majority of American municipalities.

Instead of being dominated by an economic or social elite, it is fairer to say that local politics is dominated by a *civic* elite—a group of residents who are differentiated primarily by their intense commitments to their local communities, their deep interest in local politics, and their willingness (often at considerable personal expense) to work on behalf of their neighbors. In the rancorous debate over "who governs?" it is easy to forget that most activities of elected officials are tedious and mundane. For most local politicians, there are few extrinsic rewards that can compensate for the time and effort necessary to hold office. What sustains most politicians are the *intrinsic* benefits to holding office: the idea of serving their communities or to correct a perceived injustice or problem in their communities. For this civic elite, local politics and governing are a calling. The interesting question is, in the midst of this often mundane and tedious work, what would explain the failures of current officeholders to get reelected? It is this question that we turn to next.

CHAPTER 4

Systematic versus Idiosyncratic Factors in Local Elections

IF ANYONE THINKS local government is without drama, they should just talk to Richard Cohen, mayor of Agawam, Massachusetts. For years, he had served as mayor of this rural community of about 30,000 residents that is most famous for being the home of the Six Flags of New England amusement park. Given that he had been reelected three times by large margins, it would appear most of his constituents were happy with the job he had been doing. Then came the issue of the parking lot. For years, a number of businesses that were near the amusement park had offered parking spaces for visitors at rates far below the $30 that Six Flags charged its customers. Concerned with this lost revenue opportunity, Mark Shapiro, president and CEO of Six Flags, personally lobbied Cohen and the town council to change the town code so that it would be illegal for nearby businesses to charge for parking to Six Flags customers. Citing "safety concerns," the mayor and town agreed, and soon the town began issuing fines to local businesses who opened their lots for Six Flags customers.

As one might expect, the new law generated a huge outcry among the local business owners who were affected by the ban. Not only did they argue that the parking revenue compensated for business that was lost during the summer months because of the congestion generated by Six Flags, they noted that in the twenty years they had been offering parking, not a single safety incident had occurred. Arguing that the law was simply an example of a large corporation trying to squeeze out local business, they made an effective case to the town council who reversed itself and lifted the local parking ban. This, however, was not enough to satisfy Michael Palazzi, an owner of a nearby storage facility who had

been a target of the ban. He was so incensed by the town's decision, and particularly by mayor Richard Cohen's steadfast support
of the ban, that he decided to help recruit and support Susan Dawson, a local substitute school teacher to run against him. Playing
on the popular resentment generated by the parking lot decision,
Dawson unseated Cohen by a mere 38 votes in the 2007 election.

The story and political career of Richard Cohen may have ended
there, except for a series of curious events that occurred over the
next two years. Susan Dawson, it turns out, was not very successful at managing town affairs, and her reelection bid was seriously
damaged when she was attacked by the estranged wife of a man
she was dating. The melodrama of the affair drew media attention
across the state and Dawson quickly became the subject of local
ridicule and dismay. It also provided Cohen with a second chance.
Running for reelection in 2009, he not only was able to benefit
from Dawson's personal and professional problems, but was also
able to defeat Derek Benton, his major competitor in the general
election after it was revealed that Benton had been arrested two
years earlier for an altercation with the police at a nearby strip club.

The drama of Agawam highlights a crucial irony about local
elections in the United States. Although they seldom receive much
attention and typically seem sedate, they can sometimes be quite
lively and their outcomes are notoriously difficult to predict. This
also presents something of a conundrum in trying to understand
them. Whereas political scientists have developed sophisticated
models that can forecast the outcome of presidential elections
months in advance, they have little foresight about local contests.
Partly this is because of the inherent difficulty of making generalizations about such a large number of different contests. Each
local election offers a distinct set of candidates, constituents, and
political circumstances. Elections in a poor place like Cicero, Illinois, will hinge on a different set of issues than nearby wealthy
Winnetka. In one place, Amy Gulden is campaigning against Paul
Logan, while in another place John Berg, Sam Britton, and Patty
Arndt are embattled with each other. Some local elections include
a wide range of offices from mayor to city clerk while other places
elect a small number of trustees.

How can we draw general conclusions about a class of elections that occur across so many different places, with so many different candidates, and for so many different offices? Most studies of elections are divided in their answers. On one side are those who do not even try to draw general conclusions about local elections. Journalists and historians, for example, tend to focus on the particularities of each race, such as the candidates, the particular issues of the contest, peculiarities of the community, or specific events that occur in the campaign. Scholars of big-city elections are particularly drawn to these idiosyncratic explanations because the political characteristics of most big cities seem so distinct from each other. On the other side are political scientists who seek more systematic explanations that focus on constant variables like the types of electoral institutions, the state of the economy, the social composition of a constituency, and so forth. This tendency is most evident in studies of presidential elections where the results can be accurately predicted according to a small set of predetermined variables. But even scholars of local politics often seek wide-ranging explanations that are comparable across places (Lieske 1989).

Of course, these approaches are not mutually exclusive. Any election, no matter what the office, will inevitably be influenced by *both* the particular and the systematic. What is left to be determined is the relative importance of each. And while the relative impact of factors like candidate charisma or economic conditions is well established for national elections, the importance of circumstance in local races is unknown. Thus, if we want to make predictions about local elections, we first need to determine what might be the systematic factors that shape outcomes and how much influence these factors have relative to the particular individuals, places, and circumstances.

This chapter examines the systematic factors behind local electoral results. Looking at data from over 7,000 different municipalities over a twenty-year time period, it appears that local elections are a curious mixture of the predictable and the idiosyncratic. They are predictable in that the majority of incumbents for local office either run unopposed or win reelection if they face challengers. This is consistent with the idea of managerial democracy: elections for local office should hinge on issues of custodial performance, and because incumbents get reelected at high rates, most are probably doing their jobs well enough to satisfy enough constituents or to dissuade any opponents. Identifying those instances when incumbents are likely to lose, however, turns out to be a very difficult task. Of the few identifiable trends, it appears that incumbent city council members are more likely to lose in places that are larger in size, greater in scope, and higher in bias. But the ability to predict the likelihood that any given incumbent is likely to lose, even when we know most political and social characteristics of a place, remains small. As with the case of Richard Cohen, the likelihood of winning or losing a local election seems driven more by local circumstance and idiosyncratic factors than any systematic or structural factors.

COMPARING LOCAL ELECTIONS

The first challenge to studying local elections is to figure out how to compare so many different contests. Local elections cannot be treated as identical units of analysis because each election involves distinct sets of candidates, voters, and circumstances that contribute to the peculiarities of each race. Nevertheless, if we are looking for general explanations, we need to find some basis of comparison, and when political scientists do compare large numbers of different elections, the most widely used metric is incumbency. Of all the factors used to predict electoral behavior, none is more common or powerful than incumbency. No matter if the office is a presidency or a city council position, or if the units of study are a single national election, a cross-national sample of different countries, or a comparison of legislative districts, political scientists routinely use incumbency as a central variable in their models.

The ubiquity of incumbency arises from both theoretical and empirical concerns. As noted in chapter one, most theories of voting behavior factor in the incumbents' (or the incumbents' party's) performance as a crucial predictor of electoral success. For example, retrospective theories of voting (e.g., Fiorina 1981) are based entirely on the idea of incumbent appraisal. Furthermore, incumbency itself is a powerful tool for any politician. If the single biggest hurdle that office-seekers face is making themselves known to voters, then the easiest way to overcome it is by already holding office. Outside of having lots of money, there probably is no better resource for a candidate seeking to enhance their name recognition than already being elected. Incumbents, whether they are congressmen or dog catchers, enjoy numerous advantages in publicizing themselves to citizens: they can engage in patronage or retail politics rewarding supporters with jobs or specific public services; they can attract more media attention or raise funds from interest groups during the course of the term; they can post their names on official signs and documents; they can accumulate ever-growing lists of supporters whom they can mobilize during elections. Given all these advantages, it is no surprise that incumbents at all levels of government in the United States are overwhelmingly successful.

Incumbency is also used in most empirical studies because it is one of the few metrics that is comparable across different types of elections, particularly when there are incommensurate party systems, governing institutions, or numbers of candidates.[1] For this research, incumbency will also be used as the basis of comparison across different local elections. Although this strategy limits our ability to study those elections where no incumbent is running, it will provide the most useful way of comparing what otherwise might seem figuratively like a bunch of apples, oranges, pears, and bananas.

Incumbency is also crucial to studying local elections because of the managerial character of local democracies. Since managerial democracy is less about ideological visions of how a society should be organized and more about how well it functions within the parameters of its charter, elections should hinge even more on incumbent performance than in larger, existential races. And perhaps no factor is more telling regarding the managerial character

[1] Of course, any model that uses incumbency as a central metric will not be able to predict open-seat elections (i.e., elections where no incumbent is running) particularly when they are nonpartisan or involve incommensurate party systems. This study is no exception, although the matter of open-seat elections will be taken up in further detail in chapter 5.

of local governments than the percent of officeholders who run unopposed. In existential democracies (i.e., those whose powers are broad in scope), one rarely finds unopposed elections, because there are too many groups running for ideological reasons. For example, the many communist parties of San Marino or the scores of ethnic parties in India are a continual presence on the ballot, even if they have little chance of winning, because they offer an outlet of symbolic expression for the voters. But when the office in question has very circumscribed powers or a very limited mandate, such symbolic political gestures have less salience. It is unclear what an avowedly communist candidate could do as a city council member because the municipality has no authority to socialize the means of production. Although the occasional Maoist slate might appear on the ballots in Berkeley, California, or a Tea Party candidate in Fountain Hills, Arizona, such ideological parties are much more the exception than the rule. Instead, because managerial democracy typically revolves around mundane issues like meeting budgets, service delivery, and taxes and fees being kept in check, candidates will be evaluated more on custodial competence than ideological position.

A quick look at some electoral statistics bears this conclusion out. In the 2008 general elections to the House of Representatives, fewer than 20 of the 435 members ran unopposed (and even fewer if write-in candidates are included), despite having an incumbency retention rate of over 90 percent. In other words, even though the overwhelming majority of incumbents in Congress are likely to be reelected, they almost always attract at least one opponent on the ballot. Although comparative data for all the localities in the United States do not exist, a quick look at a sample of municipal and school district elections suggests that this is decidedly not the case for local governments. For example, in 2009 there were 843 contested elections in suburban Cook County, Illinois, for offices including mayors, city council members, city clerks, treasurers, and library and school district trustees. Of these, 512 were uncontested, meaning there were as many candidates on the ballot as positions being filled. A study of school district elections in South Carolina finds similarly high rates of unopposed elections over three different time periods: of the 499 number of school district seats up for election over three years, only 256 were actually contested (Berry and Howell 2007). This corresponds with my qualitative research. In our interviews with various mayors and city council members, one of the most often-cited concerns was simply finding enough qualified people to serve much less run for local office.

The simple difficulty in staffing many locally elected offices (which typically are unpaid) coincides with the two key findings of the previous chapters. First, the people who vote in local elections tend to be stakeholders, that is, they are older homeowners who have lived in their communities for a long time. Second, politicians who run in local elections tend to be older, educated, white men who are motivated largely by a sense of civic duty and a strong attachment to their communities. Given the strong civic orientation of most candidates who seek local office and the custodial concerns of the local electorate, it is unsurprising that so many local elections go unchallenged. After all, if, as a voter, my primary concern is whether the mechanics of my locality are operating smoothly, why should I seek to fix something that is not already broken?

But local politics are not always so congenial, and the key to understanding local elections is to identify those circumstances where conflict supersedes consensus and incumbents face not only challenges but also potential defeat. Here is where the theories outlined in chapter 1 may be of some use. For just as size, scope, and bias differentiate who votes and who runs for office, they should also determine when incumbents face challengers and possibly lose elected office.

Population Size and Electoral Success

If one were running for reelection, would it better to be in a large democracy or a small one? The answer to this question depends on your prior assumptions about politics and population size. On the one hand, if you believe that personally knowing more constituents would give you an advantage and that politicians in a smaller community are probably more likely to personally know more of their voters, then a smaller place might be better for incumbents. As we saw in chapter 1, in a town of under 5,000 people that has a 20 percent turnout rate, a candidate needs to convince only 501 voters to support him or her in order to win an election. Any reasonably motivated incumbent could probably become acquainted with 501 voters during the course of a term. Of course, this smaller size might also be advantageous for the challenger as well, since convincing 501 voters to "throw the bums out" is probably a less formidable task for a political upstart than convincing 5,001.

On the other hand, if you believe that the less constituents know about their elected officials the more incumbents benefit, then a bigger-sized place may seem to provide more advantages. This, at least, is what the research suggests. Political scientist Jessica Trounstine (2008) has found that in settings with limited information about candidates, incumbents tend to do much better at getting reelected. As noted earlier, this may be due to the fact that voters in low-information situations are more likely to utilize a recognizable heuristic (i.e., ceteris paribus I'll vote for the familiar name than the unfamiliar one). Incumbents in larger places may have greater advantages because they are able to marshal the resources of their office in their favor, such as in sponsoring key pieces of legislation or having their names put on certain public works. In addition, the greater costs of running for office in a larger place may also deter many challengers. Indeed, small size may be a disadvantage to incumbents precisely because it is relatively easier for challengers to meet and mobilize voters in a smaller place than a larger one.

What is not clear is whether the personal connections to voters in smaller places are a greater benefit to incumbents than the low-information levels and greater resources in larger places. This question can be partially answered in data collected by the International City County Manager's Association (ICMA). Every five years, the ICMA surveys member municipalities with more than 2,500 residents. This chapter utilizes data from the 1986, 1991, 1996, 2001, and 2006 ICMA surveys, which were then merged with data from the 1990 and 2000 U.S. Census to get demographic information on the place In addition, the Census of Governments (a census of governmental units conducted by the federal government every five years), is used to provide information on the range of services and type of governmental structure of the community. Together, these data comprise over 7,000 different places and cumulatively provide more than 14,000 total cases. For the rest of this chapter, this study will look at those places between 2,500 and 100,000 in size that are either council-manager or mayor-council forms of governments (which make up over 96 percent of the sample).

To calculate incumbency reelection, I utilize a question in the ICMA survey, where city clerks were asked to report the number of incumbents who had run in the past election for city council and, of these, the number that were reelected. Before going further, it is important to acknowledge a major caveat: the ICMA data may be the single best source of information currently available about local governments and elections, but they do suffer from a few problems. First, because the data are based on survey forms filled out by city managers, clerks, or other administrative staff members, they are subject to human errors either in information or booking. Second, the survey only asks respondents to indicate how many incumbent city council members were running for reelection and, of those, how many won. It does not ask how many challengers were on the ballot and provides no way of knowing whether the incumbent was actually opposed. This is an especially important consideration because just as incumbents may be more likely to lose in certain kinds of places, they may also be more likely to be challenged in certain kinds of places, affecting their reelection rates. Thus any findings derived from these data must be interpreted accordingly.

With these caveats in mind, we can now turn our attention to the findings from the data. Figure 4.1 lists the percent of municipalities where at least one incumbent city council member had lost reelection by its population size. Across every year in the survey, the lowest rates of incumbent losses were consistently in the smallest places and, in three out of five years, the highest rates of incumbent losses were in the largest places. In most years, there appears to be a generally linear increase in the percent of places with incumbent city council members losing reelection and their population size.

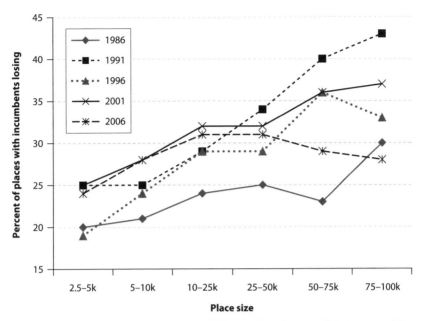

Figure 4.1. Percent of places with incumbent losses by population size 1986–2006. *Sources*: 1986–2006 ICMA, 1990 and 2000 U.S. Census (ncases = 16,748).

For example, in 1991, 25 percent of places under 10,000 in population had an incumbent lose, rising to 28 percent of places between 10,000 and 25,000 in population, 34 percent of places between 25,000 and 50,000 in population, 40 percent of places between 50,000 and 75,000, and 43 percent of places above 75,000 in size. Although such a strong linear pattern is not evident every year, the general trend appears to be quite strong: a smaller population size appears to be more advantageous for incumbents than challengers.[2]

[2] These changes are not due to relative sizes of city councils in smaller and larger places. Larger municipalities are more likely to have larger city councils, which provide more possible incumbents to be defeated, but these differences are not merely a function of city council size. When the ratio of the number of incumbents defeated relative to the city council size is used as the unit of analysis, similar differences in average scores occur across population sizes. In other words, even when taking the larger city council sizes into account, incumbents in larger places do worse than in smaller ones. Nevertheless, to minimize this possible effect, I limited the analysis in the ICMA data listed here to places with city councils under ten members in size.

So, at first glance, it looks like being in a smaller rather than larger place is better for an incumbent city council member. There is, however, a slight problem with this conclusion: a municipality's total population size is not necessarily the same as a council member's constituency size. For city council members who represent specific wards or districts, the relevant electoral size stems from their particular electoral unit and not their overall city. This is particularly the case in larger places that are more likely to have district elections. Although over 70 percent of smaller communities (places under 25,000 in size) rely solely on at-large elections for their city councils, roughly half of larger places utilize specific legislative districts for at least some of their council members. These districting arrangements also correspond with varying levels of incumbent success. Across all time periods in the ICMA sample, incumbents lost only in 24 percent of towns that had solely at-large electoral districts, whereas incumbents lost in 32 percent of towns with either all or some district-based city council seats.

These contrasting results present something of a puzzle. Holding office appears to be more difficult in a larger place than a smaller one, but, among city council members, representing a larger constituency seems to be more conducive to reelection than representing a smaller one. Part of these results may be due to advantages conveyed by council members in at-large elections. Not only do they benefit from lower levels of citizen information and higher costs faced by their challengers, they will also find it easier to link with fellow council members and run as a slate of candidates. If a candidate is running for a single district seat, the usefulness of a common slate may be mitigated and they may be forced to run as an individual candidate.

In addition, these results also may be due to the fact that smaller places are also more likely to have at-large elections than larger places. The data provide some support for this explanation. Figure 4.2 depicts the percentage of places in the ICMA data where an incumbent lost reelection by the size of the place and the type of electoral system. Although incumbents fared better in at-large elections across all categories, the biggest differences were among

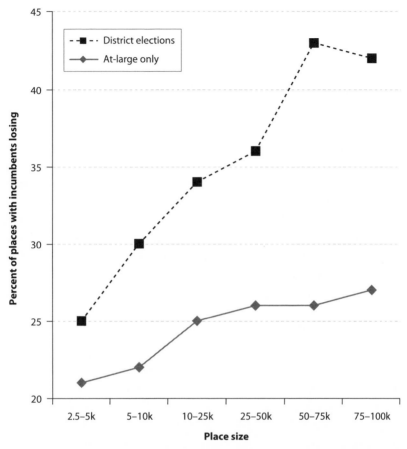

Figure 4.2. Percent of places where incumbents lost reelection by city size and type of election. *Sources*: 1986–2006 ICMA, 1990 and 2000 U.S. Census (ncases = 16,748).

the largest places. In the smallest places (between 2,500 and 5,000 in size), there is only a small, 4 percent difference in incumbent reelection success between places with at-large versus district elections. But as the size of the place grows, the difference between the two categories steadily widens. The greatest differences among places occur in the categories of the two largest population sizes. In cities over 50,000 in population, incumbents lost in only 27 percent of places with at-large elections, but in 42 percent of places with district elections.

Thus, looking just at two factors (size and electoral districting), it is better to run for reelection in a smaller place than a larger one; but, if one is seeking reelection in a larger place, it is better to represent the entire community rather than a particular district. What is not clear is whether these results are, by themselves, consistent with either hypothesis about the importance of personal connections to voters or citizen information for incumbent success. Moreover, it is also not clear how much these results are being driven by differences in running unopposed, that is, are candidates in smaller places or from at-large constituencies more likely to be reelected because they are less likely to be opposed? Unfortunately, the ICMA data do not have any other items that allow for these competing hypotheses to be tested more directly. Adjudicating these results will have to await individual-level data, as presented in chapter 5.

It is also possible that population size is not affecting these different results as much as other, unmeasured characteristics, particularly among those places that have district elections. In other words, perhaps the relationship between population size and incumbent reelection success is due to factors more common in larger places, such as their greater institutional powers or their greater economic heterogeneity.

Consider figure 4.3, which differentiates the percentage of places where incumbents lost not just by population size and at-large versus district elections, but also by their type of government (mayor-council versus council-manager governments). Adding another variable to the analysis, it appears that much of the relationship between incumbent success and population size is not influenced simply by having district elections, but also by the type of government. The impact of population size is almost negligible among places with at-large elections and council-manager governments: incumbents lost in only 4 percent more places that were over 75,000 in population than in places that were under 5,000 in size. Incumbents appeared to be most affected by population size in places with both mayor-council governments and district elections. Among this group, incumbents lost, on average, in only 28 percent of the smallest places but in roughly 45 percent of places

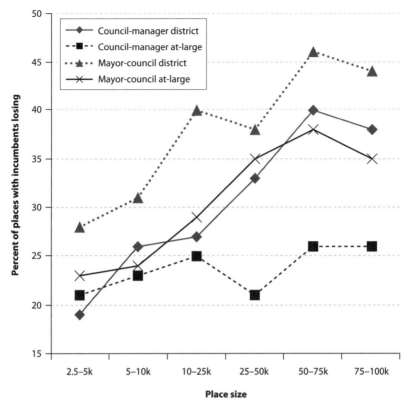

Figure 4.3. Percent of places with at least one incumbent losing by population size, form of government, and at-large versus district elections. *Sources*: 1986–2006 ICMA, 1990 and 2000 U.S. Census (ncases = 16,748).

over 50,000 in population. The other two categories (council-manager governments with district elections, and mayor-council governments with at-large elections) also showed smaller rises in incumbent losses with population growth.

Clearly then, the impact of population size cannot be considered simply by itself but must be viewed in relationship not only to the type of electoral system but also to the very structure of the governing institutions. Larger population sizes have a greater electoral impact depending on whether a city council member represents a particular district and must serve with a popularly elected mayor. To better understand the importance of institutions, it is necessary to examine the second major characteristic of local democracy: scope.

INSTITUTIONAL SCOPE AND ELECTORAL SUCCESS

As a rule, senators and governors do better at getting reelected than congressmen or state legislators. Previous research has shown that as the profile and prestige of the office grow, the rate of incumbent reelection increases (Ansolabehere and Snyder 2002). Although the greater electoral success of governors and senators may have to do with the greater visibility their offices provide, it might also have to do with their relative scope. As we have seen, democracies can be differentiated not simply by their population sizes but by the amount of power concentrated in their institutions. This can be both in the powers formally codified in their national constitutions or municipal charters and in the extent to which power is concentrated within a single executive or is widely dispersed among several competing branches. Senators and governors generally have more power than congressmen and state legislators, and this power may translate into greater electoral success. The question is whether this also holds for local office.

At first glance, it would seem unlikely that scope will be a very promising predictor of electoral success for local incumbents. Most local governments are relatively narrow in scope—their powers are strictly limited by their state charters and they are statutorily subservient to their state governments. Consequently, most municipalities will not demonstrate much variation in scope, particularly in comparison with state or national governments. That said, not all municipalities are identical either. Not only do they differ in the amount and scale of services they directly provide, but they also vary in their institutional arrangements. Some municipalities concentrate a great deal of power in the hands of an elected mayoralty while others delegate a significant amount of power to an appointed city manager, who makes most of the budget and hiring decisions.

Although such institutional differences may seem rather minor, they can have profound electoral consequences. One of the most common laments expressed by local officials during the researching of this book was the problems that came from having an expanded range of city services. Politicians in towns that had to provide their own fire, police, and road services often expressed dismay not only at the expenditures that such services extracted from their budgets, but also at the wider array of possible problems that having such services often presented. One politician privately conveyed to me a wish that her town did not get a state grant to help redevelop its central business district, largely because it was likely to stoke up so many heated political fights over how the redevelopment would occur. For a politician solely interested in reelection, having a greater range of municipal responsibility may be a liability.

On the other hand, local municipalities that are greater in scope also provide local officials with more opportunities for the types of activities that scholars of the American Congress claim are important for incumbent success, namely credit claiming. Political scientist David Mayhew (1974) famously argued that the American legislative branch is remarkably well constructed to assist its members in seeking reelection by giving them ample opportunities for directing resources to their districts and particular constituents through its committee system. By serving or chairing on certain committees, legislators are able to craft legislation that would meet particular constituent needs and thus buoy more support in the next election. The same factor also could be at work for local offices. If a municipality offers a greater array of services or if a mayor is able to draw up a budget or make most hiring decisions, each has a greater advantage in cultivating particular constituent groups. The flip side of having to offer a lot of services is to be in charge of a budget that offers many opportunities for political patronage and favoritism.

According to some simple cross-tabulations, an incumbent city council member's reelection success seems hindered by greater concentrations of executive power. Table 4.1 lists the percentages of places where an incumbent city council member lost a reelection bid by different institutional arrangements such as a council-manager versus a mayor-council form of government and, among places with a mayor, whether the mayor's position was a full-time job and if the mayor had veto power over council decisions. In all instances, a greater level of mayoral power corresponds with a higher percentage of city council incumbents losing reelection

TABLE 4.1
Percent of Places with Incumbents Losing by Types of Government

	Council-Manager Govt.	Mayor-Council Govt.	Full-Time Mayor*	No Full-Time Mayor*	Mayor with Veto Power*	Mayor No Veto Power*
Percent of Places with Incumbents Losing	24	29	35	26	30	27

Source: 1986–2006 ICMA and 1990 and 2000 U.S. Census; ncases = 16,748.

* Only municipalities with Mayor-Council forms of government.

bids. For example, incumbents lost in only 24 percent of places with council-manager governments but 29 percent of places with mayor-council governments. Among the latter group, the places where the mayor's job was a full-time position report a 35 percent rate in incumbency loss compared to only 26 percent where the mayor was not full-time. Similarly, incumbents were three percentage points more likely to lose in places where the mayor had veto power compared to places where he or she did not.

These results invite contradictory interpretations. On the one hand, incumbents may do less well in places with greater mayoral power because that mayoral power diminishes the capacities of city council members to claim credit for various government services, particularly as they cede more responsibility to the executive. On the other hand, city council incumbents also perform slightly better in places where city managers have greater powers—analysis of the 2001 and 2006 ICMA data show a five-percentage point increase in incumbent reelection success when city managers have greater responsibilities. If incumbent success hinged on credit claiming, then ceding hiring and budgetary powers to a city manager should also correspond with less electoral success in these places too. The mere fact that having a full-time mayor corresponds with such a sharp difference in reelection rates suggests that mayoral power may be representing some factor other than credit claiming in shaping electoral results.

It may be, as many politicians claim, that a mayoral system is indicative of having more municipal services, which may increase incumbent vulnerability because incumbents are forced to deal with a wider arrange of issues that stoke constituent resentment. For example, if a town is responsible for street maintenance, then incumbent city council members are likely to be blamed when potholes are not filled. The data suggest that places with a full-time mayor or greater mayoral powers also have responsibility for a greater arrange of services. Only seven percent of places that offered fewer than six local governmental services mentioned had full-time mayors compared to 16 percent of places that offered more than eight of these services.[3]

Moreover, in places that offered more of these services, incumbent city council members were less likely to be reelected. Figure 4.4 lists the percent of places where incumbents were defeated by different numbers of city services offered and whether the places had a full-time mayor. In general, incumbents did less well as the number of services directly offered increased: if we consider all three government types combined, we find that incumbents lost in less than 25 percent of places that offered two or fewer services compared to 29 percent of places that offered eight or more services. The detrimental effects of having more municipal services to incumbents are most evident in places with a full-time mayor. Where a full-time mayor serves, the electoral impact of a larger number of services grows from 25 percent for places with fewer than two services to 37 percent among places with eight or more services. In places without a full-time mayor, the percentage of places where incumbents lost increases as the number of services rises from less than two to more than four, going from 20 percent of places to 25 percent of places, but levels off after that.

Of course, these results may also be capturing other factors related to incumbent success such as population size, because larger places are also more likely to offer more municipal services. Although this possibility will be examined in greater detail below, from this simple analysis, it appears that increasing scope creates a greater liability than a benefit for incumbents. Not only are incumbents more likely to lose in places with a full-time mayor, they

---

[3] For a description of these services, see chapter 1.

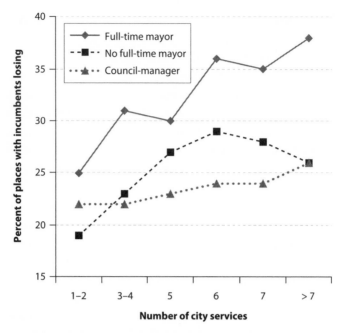

Figure 4.4. Percent of places with incumbents losing by number of municipal services offered and their type of government. *Sources:* 1986–2006 ICMA, 1990 and 2000 U.S. Census (ncases = 16,748).

are more likely to lose in places that offer more municipal services. As many local politicians I interviewed suspected, when local governments have more responsibilities, particularly in the hands of elected officials, constituents acquire more reasons to be disgruntled. Of course, once again, these results may be a function of other factors that are more common in municipalities that offer lots of services than those that do not, such as population size. However, before examining this possibility, it is necessary to examine one more factor in isolation: bias.

BIAS AND ELECTORAL SUCCESS

Six months after we first interviewed her in October of 2008, Riverdale, Illinois mayor Zenovia Evans lost her bid for reelection. When we first heard this news we were surprised. From our impression, Evans appeared to embody all of the characteristics of a successful town leader—dedicated, responsible, pragmatic, and level-headed. Although Riverdale was facing economic challenges, like many suburbs on Chicago's south side, Evans seemed to be doing most of what was in her power to address them. It was unclear what more she could do to attract jobs or deter youth delinquency given the general postindustrial decline that characterizes the area. Nevertheless, in 2009 Evans was thoroughly defeated by Deyon Dean, a former town trustee and director of a local youth services organization.

Although many factors could have contributed to Evans's defeat (Riverdale's chronic unemployment and crime levels were not helped by the ongoing recession), one important factor, ironically, appeared to be race. Riverdale has undergone a major demographic transition in the past four decades. In 1970, it was a predominantly white suburb comprising workers employed in nearby steel mills. Today, it is an overwhelmingly African American town. This demographic transformation set the stage for a new kind of politics in Riverdale. Although Evans was Riverdale's first African American mayor, Dean pressed race as an issue in regard to city hiring. Many African Americans in Riverdale expressed frustration with the fact that large percentages of the town's police and fire departments are white. Evans had long maintained cordial relationships with the policeman's union and had refused to replace many long-standing white officers with black ones simply because of their skin color. Deyon was able to utilize this issue, particularly in the context of an economic recession, to his advantage and mobilize support among younger members of Riverdale's black community who felt city resources (and locals' tax dollars) were going toward people who didn't live in a community that was so desperate for jobs.

The defeat of Zenovia Evans exemplifies a third characteristic of democracy: bias. As described in previous chapters, bias is the extent that a democracy's resources are unevenly distributed among its constituents. While local governments tend to be relatively small and limited in scope, they exhibit a much greater range in bias. Utility, library, and fire district governments, for example, are largely unbiased because they offer their services on a relatively uniform basis; school districts are high in bias because only parents and employees get the direct benefits from tax revenues that are uniformly paid by all property owners. Across the spectrum of governments, municipal governments, being general-purpose governments, should be relatively unbiased, at least in theory. Their most common services, including police and fire protection, roads, water, sewage, and waste management, should be relatively universalistic, particularly in comparison with redistributive types of programs like welfare, assistance to the elderly, or tax breaks to encourage business development. In practice, of course, even the most universalistic municipal service can be highly differentiated: potholes get filled in some neighborhoods more quickly than in others, government jobs or contracts are more likely to go to political supporters or cronies in some towns than in others, or, as in the case of Riverdale, citizens become upset because outsiders appear to be getting town jobs. In short, nearly any government activity can be performed in a biased manner.

This highlights the biggest difficulty with a concept like bias: how can one actually measure it? Without extensive resources to track specific municipal activities across the tens of thousands of local governments in the United States, it is nearly impossible to gauge firsthand how biased they are in the distribution of their resources. By itself, spending levels will not indicate bias because it is unclear whether the money is spent in a biased manner. For example, if a town hires a garbage company to haul its trash, it is difficult to know if the garbage contract was awarded on merit or on the basis of patronage. This is why factors like corruption are so notoriously difficult to pinpoint.

Given all of the difficulties in directly measuring bias, an alternative strategy is to use proximate sources. As noted in chapter 1, bias can be shaped by a community's income level, its racial composition, its patterns of property ownership, whether its political arrangements facilitate political patronage (such as having partisan elections), and its expenditure patterns, particularly if it has a high proportion of city employees. Poorer towns are more biased than wealthy ones because any hiring or contracting decisions are likely to have a more immediate economic impact on residents. Racially heterogeneous towns are more likely to be biased because of demands for proportional allocation of services by race or ethnicity, as in Riverdale. Places with heavy concentrations of commercial real estate are likely to be more biased because of the disproportionate influence of property holders seeking exchange value in local politics (Logan and Molotch 1987). Partisan elections will facilitate machine politics and political favoritism, while disproportionately high spending may indicate a system of machine politics.[4] Although each of these factors may not directly relate to bias (one may see perfectly unbiased governments in poorer, racially heterogeneous places with partisan elections), the hypotheses in chapter 1 suggest that each will increase the pressure on local politics to veer in a more biased direction.

The second challenge with the concept of bias is determining whether it is harmful or helpful to incumbents. Here again we can anticipate bias operating in a way that both favors and disadvantages incumbents. Much of the political impact of bias will relate to the extent of resource mal-apportionment, particularly in relation to a town's electoral participation. If a town's services are only slightly biased, then incumbents are unlikely to face the ire of most constituents because few people are likely to be aware of any minor imbalances in the distribution of town resources. People who live farther away from fire stations, for example, are probably no more likely to be dissatisfied with the board members of their fire district even though their fire protection is somewhat less robust than that of people who live close to fire stations. However, when municipal resources are steered toward very specific groups at the expense of others, particularly in more visible or costly ways, then constituents will begin to have stronger feelings about incumbents: beneficiaries of the bias are likely to be more fervent in their support, while those losing resources are likely to grow more hostile. Thus, as with the case of Zenovia Evans, the

---

[4] Of course, even if a city has disproportionately high spending in some areas compared to others, it may not necessarily represent a politically unpopular form of bias or even patronage; it may simply reflect the will of the citizenry to direct public resources to a particular problem.

citizens of Riverdale became indignant because they saw city jobs going to groups who were not like them.

The relatively safety of an incumbent in a biased system, therefore, hinges on his or her ability to get the beneficiaries of bias to turn out in higher numbers than the nonbeneficiaries. One of the most common ways this is done is by scheduling elections at unusual times. School districts, in particular, are notorious for picking unusual dates for bond elections—by depressing voter turnout they are able to get more parents and teachers voting relative to the general population (Moe 2005). Political scientist Jessica Trounstine (2008) finds that this works among municipalities too: incumbents do better as voter turnout declines, and in these low-turnout environments, municipal spending is directed more toward special interests.

Another important factor relating to bias in local elections is the existence of a local political organization and, in many cities, this means a political machine. Urban political machines have a long and inglorious history in the United States. Started largely in the nineteenth century, political machines were hierarchical organizations that organized large numbers of voters through political patronage—for example, by awarding jobs, city services, cash payments, and other benefits in exchange for votes. Large machines, such as Tammany Hall in New York, were quite successful at manipulating the outcome of big-city elections and holding political power. And while the glory days of the political machine may have passed, machine politics (the manipulation of political participation through direct material incentives) are still commonplace in many large American cities.

In most local elections, machine politics are far less common. Most municipalities in the United States have electoral features that are specifically designed to inhibit political patronage. For example, in the late 19th century, many suburban areas incorporated themselves and adopted "reform-style" practices precisely to keep out the perceived corruption of nearby urban bosses (Teaford 1979). By replacing mayors with councils and professional managers, eliminating council districts for at-large jurisdictions, and holding nonpartisan elections, many suburbs effectively preempted the formation of patronage organizations. So while patronage politics may still have an impact in some large cities, large-scale political machines are rare in most suburban and rural municipalities.

To test for the influence of bias in municipal elections, we can return to the ICMA data. Table 4.2 lists the percentages of places where incumbents lost, by different levels of income, racial composition, percent of the population renting their homes, whether they had partisan elections, and per capita expenditures spent on full-time employee salaries. One factor clearly related to incumbent success appears to be income, although only at the upper end of the economic spectrum. As a median household incomes rises above $50,000 a year, the rate of incumbency reelection begins to increase. Incumbents lost in only 23 percent of places with a median household income between $50,000 and $75,000 and in only 18 percent of places with a median household income between $75,000 and $100,000. And, among the very wealthiest places, incumbents lost in only 10 percent of local elections.

Race also appears to be related to incumbent success, but as with income, only at one end of the demographic spectrum. Incumbents were defeated in 41 percent of the small number of places that are less than 10 percent white in the ICMA sample; however, after this point, the rate of incumbent reelection remains mostly flat. Incumbents also fared slightly less well as the percent of renters increased in a community, although these differences are most likely a function of city size and income, as we'll see later.

Interestingly, the most obvious measure of bias, having a partisan ballot, appears to have absolutely no relationship with incumbent success. Incumbents were not reelected in the same percentage of places with partisan ballots as without. Municipal payroll levels, another possible measure of machine politics, do correspond with less incumbent success. Among places with the lowest numbers of city employees per capita, incumbents have the highest rates of reelection, seven percentage points higher than among those places in the top quartile of city employees per capita. So while having a party label on the ballot may not help or hurt incumbents, having a large municipal payroll (and thus a higher level of taxes and fees) does correspond with less incumbent success.

TABLE 4.2

Percent of Places Where Incumbents Lost Reelection by Income, Race, Percent Renter, Partisan Ballots, and Per Capita Municipal Employment

	Percent of Places in ICMA Sample for Each Category	Percent of Places with Incumbents Losing
Median Household Income (nonadjusted dollars)		
Less than $20,000	12	26
$20,000 thru $30,000	36	27
$30,000 thru $40,000	33	29
$40,000 thru $50,000	9	26
$50,000 thru $75,000	5	23
$75,000 thru $100,000	3	18
More than $100,000	1	10
Percent White		
Less than 10 Percent	1	41
10 to 25 Percent	2	29
25 to 50 Percent	7	27
50 to 75 Percent	17	29
75 to 90 Percent	24	27
More than 90 Percent	50	26
Percent Renter		
Less than 22 percent	14	24
22 to 33 Percent	35	26
33 to 46 Percent	36	28
More than 46 Percent	15	29
Elections		
Nonpartisan	76	26
Partisan	24	26
Per Capita Employee Spending		
Lowest 25 percent of sample	25	24
25 to 50 percent of sample	25	26
50 to 75 percent of sample	25	28
Highest 25 percent of sample	25	31

Sources: 1986–2006 ICMA and 1990 and 2000 U.S. Census; ncases = 16,748.

These findings do not lend themselves to any immediate conclusions about bias. Although median household income corresponds with electoral success, it does so only among the top 10 percent of places. According to the hypotheses stated earlier, one would expect equally large political effects among the lowest ranges of the economic spectrum, particularly because the electoral stakes of local elections are all the greater. Similarly, higher levels of city employment also correspond with less electoral success for incumbents, but it is not clear whether this is indicative of there being more machine politics in these municipalities or simply greater financial inefficiency and cost. The fact that partisan ballots has no impact whatsoever on incumbent reelection success suggests that machine politics are less likely to be a factor. Nevertheless, these are imprecise measures of bias at best and, as with size and scope, the results of these simple cross-tabulations may be the consequence of other unmeasured correlates. Bias may be an important factor in local electoral politics, but whether it is a major impediment or benefit to incumbents seeking reelection remains to be seen.

CONSIDERING SIZE, SCOPE, AND BIAS IN RELATION TO EACH OTHER

In the simple analyses presented so far, a strong correspondence occurs between incumbency reelection success and several measures of size, scope, and bias. Haunting these results, however, is the problem of unmeasured variables. With all of these findings, it is unclear whether they are directly influencing electoral politics or they represent some latent yet correlated factor that might correspond with incumbent electoral success. For example, population size may directly contribute to incumbency losses or it may work as a proxy measure for some other factor that also increases with population size, such as the number of services, the scope of government, or the level of urbanism. With city-level variables this is a particular concern because so many are highly correlated with one another: larger cities are more likely to have mayors, district elections, be racially and economically heterogeneous, and offer a broader array of services. In order to sort through these competing explanations, it is necessary to use more sophisticated estimation procedures, specifically mutivariate regression equations. These equations will allow for the relative impact of each variable to be seen while taking other possible factors into consideration. Such an equation will also allow for an assessment of how much overall variation in rates of incumbent reelection can be accounted for by systematic factors. Table 4.3 lists the results from five different logistic regression equations estimating whether a place had an incumbent lose in the previous election; if the city had at least one incumbent lose it was counted as a one, otherwise it was given the value of zero.[5]

The first equation examines just the impact of population size (measured with the natural log of population), a dummy variable measuring whether the city had an at-large election, and an interaction term measuring the additional impact of population size (once again measured via a natural log) among places with only at-large elections. As with all equations, it also lists dummy variables for each year the survey was administered (the year 2001 is counted as the excluded category). Consistent with the cross-tabulations, the regression equations denote a strong, statistically significant relationship between population size and incumbency loss that is greatly attenuated in places that have district elections.

The second equation examines the variables associated with the scope of an office, focusing specifically on places with mayor-council governments.[6] As in the cross-tabulations above, the regression equations show significantly diminished incumbency re-election prospects in places with full-time mayors and places with more government services; mayoral veto power does not have a

[5] Once again, this invites the problem of city council size because larger councils have more possible council positions to be contested than smaller ones. But, as with the cross-tabulations, when a ratio of number of incumbents relative to council size is used as a dependent variable, the results are nearly identical. For the sake of clarity in exposition, I am choosing the more straightforward measure.

[6] The variables in the regression equations are scaled as they are in the cross-tabulations above: dummy variables for whether the mayor had veto power, the mayor was full-time, or whether the city had a mayor-council government (council manager was again the excluded category); the number of city services was listed as a six-category variable as displayed in figure 4.3.

TABLE 4.3
Logistic Regression Predicting Likelihood of a Municipality Having an Incumbent City
Council Member Lose an Election

	Model 1	Model 2	Model 3	Model 4	Model 5
Log (Population)	.244**			.328**	
At-Large Election	.557		−.294	−1.48**	
Log (Pop.) X At-Large Election	−.103**			−.173**	−.006
Full-Time Mayor		.355**			.110
Mayor Veto Power		.055			−.099
No. City Services		.058**		−.055*	−.010
Nonpartisan Ballot			−.085	−.136	.107
Log (Med. Hse. Inc.)			−.265**	−.358**	−.569**
Log (Percent White)			−.086	-.098	−.025
Percent Renter			.023	-.020	−.124*
Muni. Employment Spending Per Cap			.067**	.048	.049*
1986	−.352**	−.503**	−.481**	−.453**	−.690**
1992	−.029	−.040	−.137**	−.265**	−.168
1996	−.238**	−.202**	−.270**	−.329**	−.301**
Constant	−2.68**	−1.09**	1.81**	.245	2.99**
Ncases	16748	6207	15368	8578	6207
Cox & Snell R-sq.	.016	.015	.009	.013	.030

Sources: 1986–2006 ICMA and 1990 and 2000 U.S. Census.

Note: Cases include only places between 2,500 and 100,000 in population size and council sizes under 10 members. Models 2 and 5 include only municipalities with mayor-council forms of government; Model 4 includes only municipalities with council-manager forms of government.

** $p < .01$, * $p < .05$

significant relationship once these other factors are considered. The third equation examines the variables associated with bias as listed in table 4.3.[7] When all the factors associated with bias are considered together, only median household income and per capita

[7] Median household income and racial percentages are measured with variables that are the natural log of these factors; partisan elections are measured as a dummy variable; percent renter and per capita municipal employment levels are measured as four-category variables corresponding to the percentages listed in table 4.3.

employment levels exhibit relationships to incumbency loss. The equations predict that incumbents are less likely to lose as median household income rises but are more likely to lose as per capita municipal employment increases·

In the fourth model, all of the variables associated with size, scope, and bias are compared in the same logistic regression model for municipalities with council manager governments. Among this group of places, four variables exhibit substantial and statistically significant relationships to incumbent loss: population size, having at-large elections, increasing numbers of public services, and median household income. Incumbents in council-manager governments generally do less well when their cities are larger and poorer, they have district and not at-large elections, and their community offers fewer public services. Somewhat different findings occur for places with mayor-council governments, as listed in Model 5. In these municipalities, incumbents also do less well in larger and poorer places, but there is no difference between members representing specific districts as opposed to the town at large. In contrast with the cross-tabulations, incumbents in mayor-council towns also do better as the percent of renters increases, which may relate to lower levels of citizen information. Increasing levels of per capita employment correspond with less incumbent success, although these differences are small. Interestingly, the remaining variables that were previously significant, such as having a full-time mayor or the number of city services available, diminish both in magnitude and statistical significance. Nevertheless, the three largest predictors of incumbent success continue to be size of municipality, government form, and household income. Finally, an overall comparison of the two equations demonstrates that incumbents in mayor-council governments are less likely to be reelected than those in council-manager governments.

Taken together, these results suggest that, for city council members, electoral politics are more contentious in less affluent, larger places with district elections, mayors, and larger numbers of city services, employees, and homeowners. The hypotheses above suggest that these are the types of contexts that are likely to stoke citizen dissatisfaction because government responsibilities are increasing, available resources are lower, and council powers are relatively diminished. In such places, council members may be less likely to be elected because they are facing more responsibilities with less power and fewer resources.

Before accepting this conclusion, however, two important caveats must be acknowledged. First, some of these findings could be capturing an endogenous relationship between electoral politics and government services. In other words, the causal relationship between incumbent success and city services, employment, and income may not run in a simple one-way direction but may be reciprocal: city services and employment may be higher in places where incumbents are more likely to lose because these places are more electorally competitive and city council members try to increase government expenditures as a means of staying politically viable. Further analysis suggests this may be the case. When a variable measuring whether the town has term limits for its mayor is added to the equation, the relationship between city services, employment levels, and incumbent reelection attenuates and loses statistical significance; meanwhile, the equations predict that city council members are more likely to be reelected in places where mayors have term limits than in places where they do not.

Second, and most importantly, the logistic regressions not only show the impact of variables in relationship to each other, but also demonstrate how much overall predictive power the variables provide in explaining what types of places incumbents are likely to lose elections in. This often neglected statistic (indicated as a Cox and Snell R-squared) is particularly important in this case because it shows to what extent local electoral results are the product of systematic factors that are measured by the variables in the equation as opposed to other factors not measured. The fit of all the equations in table 4.3 is quite low. Even the fully specified equation in Model 5 can explain no more than 3 percent of the variance between places where incumbents lose and where they do not. Given the theoretical importance of these variables, this is a remarkably low level of explanatory power. The fact that a municipality's size, governmental forms, service and employment levels, income, and racial composition account for so little difference in whether incumbents lose suggests that local elections are probably driven more by idiosyncratic factors such as a candidate appeals, local political circumstances, or random events.

Conclusion

Like many unseated incumbents, Tom Jester never saw it coming. For years he dutifully served, and was continually reelected, as a trustee for the historically Republican suburb of Deerfield, Illinois. And to him, his repeated electoral successes were not surprising. Politics in Deerfield were generally congenial and the board of trustees had worked hard to keep the town in good shape. Even though he was a life-long Republican, Jester governed in what he thought was a largely nonpartisan manner and he had little sense of dissatisfaction from his constituents. Yet, in 2002 he and all of his fellow Republican trustees were unceremoniously thrown out of office.

At first, Jester's electoral loss seemed a complete mystery. He had not endorsed any new or controversial town projects. Deerfield was in sound fiscal condition. Nor were there any personal scandals that would stoke voter ire. So, if he was doing such a good job, why did he lose? It took some time, but after looking at the election results it became apparent to Jester that his defeat was due to forces almost entirely beyond his control. Over the past two decades, Deerfield had undergone a quiet transformation as thousands of younger, Democratic families replaced an aging generation of Republicans who had populated the suburb since the 1950s. Simply by virtue of his party affiliation, Jester was now out of sync with a majority of his constituents. As luck would have it, in 2002, the local elections coincided with a special school district election that mobilized thousands of these younger, Democratic residents who previously had never bothered to vote in town elections. When faced with choices between two sets of candidates they knew little about, the voters selected the Democrats, and Jester was thrown out of office.

Local elections are a curious mixture of the mundane and the unexpected. For the overwhelming majority of local elections, incumbents are likely to win. This is because they either run unopposed or because they are able to convince voters that they are doing a good enough job to stay in office. All things being equal, the single most powerful predictor of whether someone will win an election is whether they are already in office. Yet for all their advantages, incumbents do not always win. The ICMA data suggest that in any given year at least one incumbent city council member will lose an election in about one quarter of all municipalities. This number grows higher for places that are large in size, that are lower in income, and that have strong mayors, greater municipal responsibilities, and district elections for council members. For a local politician, reelection becomes more hazardous as one's responsibilities grow, resources and powers diminish, and opponents have easier access to mounting challenges.

These factors also explain why incumbents generally do so well. For the overwhelming majority of locally elected officials, the conditions that threaten incumbents are rarely present. Most American municipalities are council-manager governments, under 50,000 in population, and have professional city managers who take executive responsibilities under the council's authority. These places tend to provide a limited number of direct services and elect their council members at large. The governing structure of most American municipalities corresponds with a high level of electoral success.

Given that the structure of most localities coincides so well with incumbents' reelections, it is not surprising that the most of common factors that differentiate America's municipalities can tell us very little about when incumbents are likely to be unseated. Indeed, most city council members continue to be reelected in even the largest, poorest, and most administratively burdened cities, while incumbents still lose in the richest, smallest, and least-expansive towns. The sheer variety in the types of American communities, politicians, and local circumstances greatly undermines the predictive power of any general model. Unlike presidential elections, whose outcomes are greatly influenced by factors such as economic growth and partisan identification, the outcomes of local elections simply cannot be determined by large-scale, systematic variables. Thus, to better understand what shapes voting in these contests, it is important to look at the behavior of individual voters. It is this that we turn to next.

CHAPTER 5

What Influences Local Voters' Electoral Choices?

VOTERS IN PARTS OF COOK COUNTY, Illinois, periodically find a curious item on their ballots: a candidate named Jerry "Iceman" Butler. "Iceman" is not a name one often sees on a ballot. To those who don't know Jerry Butler, they may be forced to wonder "Who is this 'Iceman' and why does he have this nickname? Was he a sports star? Or maybe a mob assassin? Would having a nickname like 'Iceman' make him a better commissioner or a worse one? Should I vote for him simply because his name is 'Iceman'?" The mind reels. In truth, Jerry Butler was a very successful singer and songwriter in the 1960s and part of a soul band called "The Impressions." He has been a political fixture on the South Side of Chicago since the 1980s and is firmly rooted in Chicago machine politics. Nevertheless, he keeps listing his nickname of "Iceman" on the ballot and, given his continued reelection, it seems to be working for him.

For most Americans, the story about the "Iceman" may sound familiar. Given the sheer number of elections and variety of offices we are asked to vote on, it is not uncommon to decide between two or more entirely unknown candidates. In most of these instances, people either employ some heuristic like partisanship or use some arbitrary criteria to make a decision (such as picking a name that sounds familiar or randomly choosing the first name here and the second name there). Or some of us simply choose not to vote at all. Yet this situation creates quite a conundrum for a democracy. After all, can a system really be called democratic if citizens do not know anything about whom they are voting for? If one votes for a county commissioner simply because his name is "Iceman," what does this mean for the legitimacy of popular sovereignty?

In order to answer these questions, we need to first determine how much people know about the candidates they are choosing between and on what basis they are making their electoral choices. So what do Americans know about politics and how do they vote? The answer to this question depends on the office in question. We actually know quite a lot about how people vote for president or their congressional leaders. In fact, a person's partisanship, the state of the economy, and the candidates' stances on a few key issues can account for most people's presidential or congressional voting decisions. But what is less clear is whether people use these same criteria when voting for a city council member or water commissioner. From the evidence in the previous chapters, we know that local voters are likely to be stakeholders in their communities and that most of the candidates they are choosing from are older, long-term residents who are primarily driven by a sense of civic duty. We also know that most local elections tend to be referenda on incumbent performance and typically incumbents will do quite well. But beyond these facts, we know very little about the mental processes of local voters, such as how much information they have about local politics and candidates, whether partisanship or issues drive their electoral decisions, and how their voting calculus may vary with the size, scope, and bias of their communities.

This chapter examines what individual voters know about local elections and what factors shape their voting choices. After reviewing how and why we might expect that local voting behavior may differ from presidential voting behavior, we examine a unique dataset of over 1400 voters in 30 different smaller communities that focuses on these questions in particular. In line with their "homevoter" identities, most local voters typically have high knowledge levels about candidates and express a great deal of interest in local affairs. But because of this, local voters tend to employ different criteria than national ones. They are far more likely to base their votes on specific issues or incumbent performance and less likely to utilize heuristics like partisanship, candidate charisma, or even a memorable nickname like "Iceman," although this varies somewhat with the size, scope, and bias of their community. Nevertheless, voting for the "Iceman" is probably more characteristic of someone in a state or national election (or even in a large place like Cook County, Illinois) than the typical voter in a small-scale or local contest. Local voters, it turns out, are more likely to embody the normative expectations of the informed and rational citizen of classical democratic theory. To better appreciate this point, let us first review what we know about how people vote.

WHAT PRESIDENTIAL ELECTIONS CAN (AND CAN'T) TELL US ABOUT LOCAL ELECTIONS

Most of our knowledge about the way ordinary people vote comes from the vast literature on presidential elections. Ever since pollsters started taking scientific surveys of the American public in the 1940s, electoral scholars have focused almost entirely on national contests. This preoccupation has not gone unrewarded. Over the past sixty years, an enormous body of research has emerged on the determinants of presidential vote choice. Not only can political scientists usually predict who is likely to win a presidential or congressional race months before they happen, but they can also predict how any given citizen is likely to vote, once they know a few key pieces of information such as his or her partisanship, race, gender, and evaluations of the incumbent regime. Given this treasure trove of research, presidential elections would seem to be a good place to start when looking to explain how individuals vote in local elections.

The problem with such a common sense strategy is that the principal factors that drive presidential voting (namely partisanship, candidate charisma, and retrospective evaluations of economic conditions) may not always be relevant in local elections. In fact, the closer we look at the primary drivers of presidential vote choice, the less applicable to local contests they appear to be. Take the example of partisanship. The most important and enduring determinant of presidential vote choice is what party a person belongs to. Ever since the publication of *The American Voter* (Campbell et al.

1960), partisan affiliations have been recognized as *the* central factor in shaping Americans' presidential voting behavior. Acquired early in life and being remarkably enduring, people's partisan attachments exert a tremendous impact on the political perceptions and vote choice (Green, Palmquist, and Schickler 2004). All things being equal, Republicans are far more likely to vote for Republican candidates and Democrats for Democratic candidates. But partisanship doesn't merely predict vote choice, it also shapes the way voters assess information and perceive the political world—self-identified Republicans, for instance, are far more likely to assume that Republican candidates share their views on various issues (even if they don't), to better appraise the performance of a Republican incumbent, or to discount negative information about other Republicans (Bartels 2002). Partisanship continues be the primary lens through which Americans comprehend politics, at least, at the national level.

For most local elections, however, partisanship is irrelevant. The biggest reason is the simple fact that most municipalities have nonpartisan elections. In fact, over 75 percent of municipal elections in the United States are officially nonpartisan (Wood 2002). Although nonpartisan elections do not necessarily preclude the formation of local political organizations, when such groups do arise, they tend to be parochial coalitions of local groups or slates of candidates that have little relationship to the national parties (Lee 1960). Partisanship may also be less important in local elections because of the limited scope of most municipalities. Zoning, services, property taxes, land-usage, traffic, and redevelopment are the primary staples of local politics, but these do not easily map onto the agendas of the national Republican or Democratic parties. Furthermore, many municipalities are quite socially homogeneous (see chapter 2), and it is unclear whether they would have a wide variation on party preferences among their residents. In the absence of a party moniker or in the context of such political homogeneity, what becomes one of the most salient cues for voters, the biggest divider of the citizenry, and a fundamental predictor of vote choice, is often immaterial.

Of course, American voters do not solely vote along party lines. Indeed, one of the most powerful critiques of the partisan-centered model of vote choice comes from scholars who see voting as a more instrumental behavior (Key 1966; Fiorina1981; Kiewiet and Rivers 1984). According to this "rational choice" perspective, people vote for those candidates who mostly closely adhere to their policy preferences. Yet, as most scholars are quick to note, this simple theory faces an immediate complication: many voters don't have definitive preferences and, even if they do, they probably do not have the time or energy to figure out which candidates are closest in opinion to themselves (Zaller 2004). In fact, given that the odds they could cast a decisive vote are so low relative to the inconveniences of voting, voting itself is a largely irrational act (Oliver and Wolfinger 1999).

But the biggest challenge to the idea that Americans vote according to a set of policy preferences is the simple fact that most Americans know very little about public affairs. For example, a majority cannot identify the Speaker of the House, their local congressional member, or the Chief Justice of the Supreme Court (Delli Carpini and Keeter 1997). And if Americans are uncertain about basic political *facts*, they are even fuzzier when it comes to political *issues*. Even though the national media is filled with stories about most major political issues, the American citizenry remains notoriously underinformed about most national policies or the candidates' stances on them, and only a small percentage of Americans demonstrates any type of consistency in their political opinions (Converse 1964; Ansolabehere, Rodden, and Snyder. 2008).

Some scholars have tried to salvage the rationality of ordinary voters by looking at cognitive shortcuts known as heuristics, the general rules of thumb that help an underinformed person make a reasonable choice. A classic example of a heuristic is the popularity heuristic: in trying to decide between two unknown restaurants, it is better to choose the one with the most people because presumably other people know something more about its quality. One common heuristic in voting is a candidate's party affiliation. I may not know very much about the specific stance of a Democrat,

Republican, Libertarian, or Green Party candidate, but based on his or her party affiliation I can probably make a good guess about where this person will stand on issues.

In presidential elections, retrospective evaluations of incumbent performance are often viewed as another important determinant of vote choice: if incumbents are doing well, voters will continue to support them; if not, they will "throw the bums out." Past research has demonstrated that such retrospective evaluations are a powerful predictor of vote choice. If unemployment or inflation rise, or economic growth subsides, or a country is in an unpopular war, incumbent presidents (or their fellow party members) face a much steeper task in convincing voters to keep them in office (Aldrich, Sullivan, and Borgida 1989; Nadeau and Lewis-Beck 2001).

Yet, as with partisanship, the applicability of this retrospective model for local elections is unclear. To begin with, voters usually base their retrospective evaluations more on sociotropic concerns than their own individual welfare (Alvarez and Nagler 1998; Kiewiet and Rivers 1984). In other words, a voter will blame an incumbent president if the national unemployment rate rises but will not blame the president if he loses his own job. In national elections, such sociotropic concerns typically revolve around issues of "peace and prosperity." When the economy is good and peace is at hand, incumbents tend to do well. But for most local elections, the sociotropic barometers are less self-evident. It is not that voters support irresponsible incumbents or refuse to vote relative to their mayor or council members' past behavior, but it is simply unclear which criteria they use to judge their performance. For example, unlike the case with presidential elections, it is doubtful that voters will hold their local council officials accountable for the deteriorating economy, unsuccessful wars, or other factors that may seem beyond the community's control. Some evidence suggests that local economic circumstances, such as a deflated real estate market, may be harmful to incumbents (Mondak, Mutz, and Huckfeldt 1996), but these findings are inconclusive. And while some locally elected officials have specific responsibilities, such as overseeing mosquito zones or school boards (Berry and Howell 2007), many mayors and council members are responsible for a wide range of small tasks. Barring a particular scandal or some egregious behavior, it is difficult to specify any one metric of incumbent performance that would hold across all suburbs at all times.

The third major factor in presidential voting concerns the personal qualities of the candidates themselves. A candidate's charisma and likeability have an enormous impact on people's voting behavior. Indeed, candidate likeability may simply be another heuristic that voters use when making decisions. In other words, not knowing where a candidate stands on the issues, people will simply vote for the candidate they personally *like* better. But this seemingly self-evident proposition actually raises a thorny set of empirical questions. Do people like candidates purely for their own personal charisma, or because they are from certain parties or even because of their issue positions? In other words, do I like candidate John McCain because he shares my opinions on certain issues or do I hold opinions about certain issues because of how much I like John McCain? Seeking to disentangle this reciprocal causality, political scientists have employed sophisticated statistical models to parse out the effects of partisanship, issue positions, and candidate appraisals (e.g., Markus and Converse 1979). They report that candidate evaluations trump even partisanship or issue considerations as the primary determinant of voter choice. In other words, even though a voter may disagree with Barack Obama on the issue of gay marriage or even be a Republican, she may still vote for him simply because she likes him personally better than John McCain.

But while candidate evaluations may loom large in presidential contests, their impact on small-scale elections is less clear. The biggest obstacle for most local candidates is simply getting *any* public attention. News organizations rarely focus on local elections and few candidates have the necessary campaign funds to purchase the television advertisements so important for increasing their visibility. Most election guidebooks stress the importance of yard signs and fliers for increasing the name recognition of local candidates, but it is unclear whether this name recognition is sufficient for generating a positive evaluation. As most Americans cannot correctly recall the names of challengers in their congressional elections (Jacobson 1978), it seems unlikely that they could recall who is on their local township board or their municipal clerk much less a condo board member or the treasurer of their local garden club (although more on this in a moment).

The one exception to the invisibility of local candidates, at least in big-city elections, is race. One of the most consistent predictors of urban voting behavior is the race and ethnicity of the voter and the candidate (Kaufman 2004). To understand this point, it is important to put American elections in some historical context. Until quite recently, racial and ethnic minorities were effectively excluded from being serious contenders for most presidential, senate, and gubernatorial offices. This was not the case, however, in cities. Ever since the rapid expansion of America's immigrant urban population, race and ethnicity have been crucial factors delimiting local politics. Long before a Kennedy, Giuliani, Lieberman, or Obama ran for national office, there were Irish, Italians, Jews, and African Americans being elected to mayor, city councils, and other local positions. In fact, the ethnic-based social networks were vital for coordinating patronage in most machines (Erie 1998). Ethnic social networks operating through clubs, taverns, churches, and neighborhoods were crucial mechanisms for coordinating the flow of patronage benefits. Following the Civil Rights movement of the 1960s, group-based electoral conflict began to outstrip partisan or ideological conflict in a number of large cities. Voters began to evaluate candidates for big-city offices first and foremost relative to their race and, from that, extrapolated ideas of group-related benefits that would be conferred (Browning, Marshall, and Tabb 2003). In big cities, the racial identity of both candidates and voters has become, by most indications, the most powerful predictor of vote choice (Kaufmann 2004; Hajnal 2007).

But while race and ethnicity undoubtedly have a large impact in many big-city elections, their influence for most local elections is not so clear. Most large American cities are racially diverse and many, such as Los Angeles, Chicago, Detroit, Houston, and Atlanta have an outright majority of nonwhite voters; most small municipalities, however, are racially homogeneous. Data from the 2000 U.S. Census indicate that among local governments (i.e., places under 100,000 in population), 50 percent are at least 95 percent white and 66 percent are over 90 percent white. When the only voters in an election are of one race or ethnicity, then racial politics should be irrelevant.

Of course, not *all* small towns are racially uniform. For example, much of the recent growth in suburban areas has come from minorities and particularly immigrants from Asia and Latin America. The new racial complexity of suburbia, however, raises a novel set of political questions: do racial or ethnic politics operate in a similar manner in a small, reform-style suburb as they do in a large city? Do Asian Americans or Latinos behave like other ethnic groups regarding local politics or do they depoliticize their racial or ethnic identities in a suburban context? Given all of the institutional differences between suburbs and big cities, the dynamics of minority politics in smaller cities and towns are difficult to anticipate.

The final major factor driving presidential vote choice is the candidates' stances on specific issues. Although the average American voter may be largely ignorant of public affairs or candidate positions on many policies, there are some "easy" issues that stand out and can be singularly determinative for a particular voter (Carmines and Stimson 1980). Abortion, gun rights, stem-cell research, Israel, gay marriage, and the environment are the types of issues that often motivate American voters to support a particular candidate or political party. Indeed, such issues are often at the center of presidential campaigns as candidates seek "wedge" issues to divide support among the opposition and gain a particular advantage over their rivals (Hillygus and Shields 2008).

Issues are undoubtedly important for local politics too, but their impact on local voting is hard to predict. On the one hand, we might question whether issues have a large role in local politics simply because of the circumscribed nature of local governance. Because of their limited scope, few local governments encounter the chronic challenges that ignite citizen fervor on the national level. There may be the occasional uproar over an episodic event like a proposal to expand a parking lot or to build a shopping mall, but in local politics there are few "easy" issues like abortion rights or gay marriage, which are so readily apparent in national politics. Furthermore, where these issues do arise, they tend to be limited to a particular place. For example, many communities are divided between some homeowners and real estate speculators over property development, but these battles are typically limited to more affluent communities.

On the other hand, issues might actually be more important in local elections because of turnout differences among the more politically engaged. One reason why issues are so surprisingly weak as a predictor of voting behavior is because the average voter in a presidential election is someone who does not follow politics very closely. Indeed, this is one of the reasons why partisanship is so decisive in shaping presidential and congressional voting—because Americans know so little about national issues, they typically rely on heuristics like partisanship to guess the policy stances of various candidates (Bartels 1996).

But if most Americans are so uninformed about high-profile national issues, then why would they be more knowledgeable about issues in regard to their municipalities, particularly in those places without any local media coverage? After all, most American towns do not have their own newspapers or television channels, and the sources of information about local issues are often hard to find. Furthermore, even if voters can overcome information shortfalls, it is unclear how well citizens can recognize the local candidates' positions on such pedestrian issues as zoning ordinances, bond issues, road maintenance, and so forth (Lowery and Lyons. 1989; Teske et al. 1993). Local municipalities may have important issues that are decided through elections, but there are still good reasons to doubt whether the average *citizen* can connect his or her opinions about these vital issues to a particular candidate.

The answer to this question may arise from the selective differences in participation. Because turnout in local elections is often so small and primarily involves stakeholders in a community, the average voter in a local election is likely to be someone with a high level of interest and information about local affairs. In short, issues may be more important for local elections (particularly when they are contested), precisely because such a small portion of the electorate is actually voting and because partisanship, candidate personality, and the criteria for retrospective evaluations are hard to identify.

The importance of issues relative to factors like party, race, and candidate charisma will also vary in regard to the size, scope, and bias of the locality. As we've seen in previous chapters, because they live in municipalities of small size, limited scope, and low bias, most local voters are less likely to look to cues such as partisanship, ideology, or group affiliations—the identifiers that determine national vote choices. But although the differences among localities in these dimensions is not nearly as great as the difference between all localities and the national government, there are nonetheless some variations in size, scope, and bias among localities as well, as we saw in chapter 4.

These smaller differences may also exert some influences on how local citizens vote. For example, voters in a town of 2,000 people are probably more likely to personally know at least one candidate than in a town of 20,000, and they are also more likely to be immediately connected to specific issues. If I live in a small town and the town decides to allow a commercial property development, it is probably more likely to affect me personally than if I live in a much larger place simply because of the greater proximity of all voters in a smaller community. Similarly, if my local government has a larger number of responsibilities or if power is more directly concentrated in the hands of an elected official, the candidates' stances on issues are going to have a lot more bearing on the types of public services I receive. Thus, we should expect that issues become more important and elections more contentious as the scope or bias of a local government increases.

To summarize, because few local elections have party labels on ballots, clear indicators of incumbent performance, or media-driven candidates, it is unlikely that voters in local contests will behave exactly like they do in presidential elections. While these factors will probably have *some* influence over local voting, *how* much influence will depend on a host of other factors. First, if local elections are populated mostly by stakeholders or "homevoters," then factors like salient issues may be more crucial in the calculus of local voters than our deductions above would suggest. In other words, when only the most informed and interested segments of the electorate turn out to vote, people in local elections may end up voting in a similar manner to people in higher-profile contests. Second, the impact of partisanship, issues, and candidate likeability also may vary with the size, scope, and bias of the locale. Voters in larger municipalities are probably more likely to rely on heuristics like party or candidate appeal; voters in places greater in scope are probably going to be more motivated by particular issues than in places more narrow in scope; voters dealing with highly biased governments (like school boards) are more likely to vote according to specific group interests. In order to explore these ideas, we need to ascertain first what local voters actually know about the elections they are voting in. For this, we now turn to some data.

DATA ON LOCAL ELECTIONS

Because scholars and survey organizations are mostly preoccupied with national, congressional, or even big-city elections, surveys of individual voters in smaller places are almost nonexistent. In fact, in the data archives of the Inter-university Consortium for Political Science Research, there is not a single dataset that examines voting in small-scale elections. The *only* data set that looks at individual voting behavior across a large number of smaller places is the Study of the Suburban Voter (SSV), a survey of voters from thirty different suburban municipalities across five different states (California, Georgia, Illinois, New Jersey, and North Carolina) in the period immediately following their local elections in 2004 and 2005.

The SSV data provide a number of noteworthy characteristics important for analyzing local voting behavior. Despite examining only thirty places, the communities sampled from demonstrate a wide variability in social composition and political institutions. For example, nine of the thirty municipalities had partisan elections and fifteen had mayoral elections (with the other fifteen electing only council members). The population size of the communities ranged from 1,191 in Colma, California, to 97,687 in Edison, New Jersey. The median household income of the communities varied from a low of $35,322 in Union City, Georgia, to $146,537 in Oak Brook, Illinois. The racial composition of the municipalities also varied widely, with seven predominantly white (i.e., 80 percent or more) places, fourteen places with a white plurality, four places that were majority African American, and one place with a majority of Asian Americans. Four of the places were at least 30 percent Latino, and six were at least 20 percent Asian American. Ten places in California had elections concurrent with the presidential election in the fall of 2004, while the others had their elections in 2005.[1]

Because the SSV sampled only among registered voters and only interviewed those who had reported voting in the previous *local* election, the demographic composition of the study is distinct from that of the general population. Comparing the survey sample with 2000 Census data on each of the places, the differences between the survey respondents and the general population of their communities tend to replicate the differences between voters and nonvoters as illustrated in chapter 2. The respondents in the SSV survey are better educated, more likely to be homeowners, are older, and are disproportionately white: on average, 25 percent of the residents have a college degree, compared to 45 percent of the SSV sample; 68 percent of the residents are homeowners, compared to

---

[1] Once the cities were selected, a phone survey was conducted by the Roper polling firm among randomly selected lists of registered voters. All interviews were conducted by telephone (CATI) at interviewing facilities during November 3–24, 2004, April 6–22, 2005, and November 11–29, 2005. Each interview took approximately ten minutes, on average, to administer. In the Fall 2004 and Fall 2005 waves, the sample was drawn on an "nth" name basis from lists of registered voters maintained by and purchased directly from the counties surveyed. In the Spring 2005 wave, lists were used in most selected cities, but random digit dial (RDD) was used in three communities (Deerfield, Oak Park, and Sauk Village) because such lists were not available for their respective counties. In twenty-seven of the thirty suburbs, interviews were conducted until fifty respondents were gathered. In three places, however, the small size of the community precluded that ability to gather all fifty interviewees. Cooperation rates were 22 percent for Fall 2004, 14 percent for Spring 2005, and 20 percent for Fall 2005. These low rates were largely attributable to the small portion of voters in the respective communities.

85 percent of the SSV sample; the median age of the population in the communities is 36, whereas the median age of the SSV sample is 54; and 60 percent of the residents are white, compared to 82 percent of the SSV sample, while as a corollary, nonwhite residents are generally underrepresented in the Census data.

Despite these differences, the sample appears to be representative of the *voters* in each of these jurisdictions, because the distribution of reported vote choice among the SSV sample generally reflects the actual distribution of votes in each election. For example, 161 out of 165 council candidates in the SSV had reported vote percentages that were within 10 percentage points of the actual vote percentages they had received; 146 out of 165 candidates had reported vote percentages within 6 percentage points. Thus, while the SSV sample may not be representative of the general population of the communities that were surveyed, it appears to be representative, at least by the barometer of vote choice, of the voters in each community.

Another caveat about the SSV data is that they sampled only voters in suburban municipalities; the SSV data do not sample from rural communities. Given this fact, one may question whether the findings of the SSV data can be generalized to nonsuburban municipalities. Although this is a legitimate concern, it is not clear that rural voters are distinctive from suburban ones. Given the exposure of rural residents to mass media and the expansion of many metropolitan areas, it is difficult to presuppose that rural residents are categorically different than suburban ones. Empirical research suggests that in terms of voting behavior and political interest, rural voters are influenced more by factors such as the size of their town than by whether their town is within or not within a metropolitan area (Oliver 2001; Knoke 1977). But social scientists have found few distinctive effects of living in a rural area on political behavior that cannot be ascribed to individual-level differences in education or age. Given the absence of differences, there are no reasons to believe, a priori, that the findings from the SSV would not be replicated if these communities were further distanced from large metropolitan centers.

LOCAL ELECTORAL CULTURE

In each of the thirty localities surveyed in the SSV, respondents were asked a series of questions about their familiarity with each of the council candidates (and mayoral candidates where applicable) and some questions about their interest and feelings about local politics.[2] If the SSV data are indicative of local voters across the country as a whole, it is clear that local voters have a relatively high level of interest in and familiarity with local politics. About 46 percent of the respondents say they knew "a lot" or "a fair amount" about one or more council candidates. Although not listed, over half of the SSV respondents who lived in towns with mayoral elections knew this much about one of the mayoral candidates. Roughly a third (34 percent) of the respondents personally knew a city council candidate, a rate that was roughly the same in mayoral elections. Not surprisingly, over three-quarters of the respondents rated themselves as either somewhat or very interested in the local campaign. Local voters were also highly mobilized: about 50 percent said they had been contacted by a party, candidate, or some other organization urging them to vote in a particular way. Almost 90 percent said that the biggest problem or problems facing their community were also important in influencing their vote choice. Given the nature of the sample and the

[2] The interviewer said, "I'm going to read the names of some candidates who ran in the last election. After I say the name, I'll ask you a few questions about him or her. First is [Candidate Name]. How much would you say you know about that candidate? Would you know a lot, a fair amount, only a little, only know the name, or never heard of [Candidate]?" If the respondents had never heard of the candidate, the questioner would move to the next candidate. If the respondents had heard of the candidate, they were asked 1) if they liked him or her as a person, 2) if they agreed with him or her on the issues, 3) if they knew him or her personally, 4) if they were in the same political party as the candidate, and 5) if they voted for the candidate. The respondents were also asked questions of how interested they were in the political campaign (very interested, somewhat interested, not very interested, or completely uninterested) and whether anyone from an organization or a candidate contacted them about supporting a particular local candidate during the campaign. Finally, respondents were asked a series of open-ended questions about the most important problems facing their community (they could list up to two). They were then asked follow-up questions as to whether that problem was an important issue in influencing their voting.

responses to these items, it would appear that the typical local voter (at least as represented in the SSV sample) is someone who is politically active, fairly knowledgeable about local politics, connected to local political networks, and concerned about some particular issues. Of course, there is an inherent problem with such generalizations: what does it mean to call any one person a typical local voter? Consider, for example, just the differences in political attitudes by some of the measures of size, scope, and bias used in the previous chapters. Table 5.1 lists the average levels of political engagement by factors like population size, types of government, election timing, partisan ballots, median household income, and racial diversity. Among these variables, the largest and most consistent differences in political engagement occur by population size. Voters in smaller places are generally more interested in politics, more likely to recognize local candidates, and more likely to know a candidate personally. For example, comparing residents in places under 15,000 in population to those over 30,000 in size, we find a nine-percentage-point increase in average political interest, a ten-point increase in average candidate name recognition, and a twenty-point increase in average acquaintance with a city council candidate. Residents of smaller places are also more likely to be mobilized by a political organization or candidate.

Voters also appear to be differentiated by the scope of their local governments. Constituents in places with mayoral elections are more likely to be interested in politics, mobilized by local campaigns, and assert that issues are important for their vote choices. A similar pattern occurs when comparing places whose elections were concurrent with national elections and those places with nonconcurrent elections. Concurrent elections are likely to include a lot of voters who would not normally turn out for a local contest, and thus one might expect lower levels of information and engagement. This is what the data show. On almost every measure of political engagement, voters in places with nonconcurrent elections were more likely to be interested, mobilized, or motivated by issues.

Next we can compare voters relative to the bias of their localities. Given the limited range in potential bias among the thirty

TABLE 5.1
Differences in Political Interest, Mobilization, and Information by
Characteristics of the Place

	Very or Somewhat Interested in Local Politics	Know a Lot or a Fair Amount about City Council Candidates	Know a Council Canidate Personally	Were Contacted by Local Organizations	Agree that Local Issues Influenced Vote Choice
Population Size					
Less than 15,000	79	52	44	52	89
15,000–30,000	76	43	28	55	88
More than 30,000	70	41	24	46	91
Mayoral Election					
No	71	48	35	45	85
Yes	80	45	34	55	94
Partisan Ballot					
No	75	48	35	47	89
Yes	78	43	33	58	90
Concurrent Election					
No	78	47	38	54	92
Yes	70	44	26	44	83
Median Household Income					
Under $50,000	77	44	30	44	90
$50,000 to $100,000	75	47	32	54	91
Over $100,000	74	48	37	47	85
Racial Diversity (IQV)					
Very Homogeneous	74	48	35	55	87
Somewhat Mixed	75	48	38	52	92
Very Diverse	77	43	29	46	87
Sample Average	76	46	34	50	90

Source: The 2004–2005 Study of the Suburban Voter (SSV).

Note: Numbers in the table are percentages; the total number of cases is 1,468.

towns in the SSV sample, one would expect few differences in political engagement along this dimension. What is most surprising, however, is how little impact the proxy measures of bias (i.e., partisan ballots, median household income, and racial composition) have in relation to their residents' political engagement. Voters in places with partisan ballots are more likely to be mobilized to vote, voters in the wealthiest places are more likely to personally know candidates, and voters in the most racially diverse places are also less likely to know candidates or be mobilized. But beyond these particular instances, there are no significant differences in reported levels of political interest or issue-based voting across these three proxy measures of bias.

Of course, some of these place-level differences may be attributable to the different types of people who live in these various towns; in other words, most people who live in affluent places tend themselves to be affluent or educated. Table 5.2 lists differences in political engagement by the following individual-level characteristics; education, homeownership, length of residence in the community, and race. Consistent with the findings in chapter 2, educated voters, homeowners, and, to a lesser extent, long-term residents are more likely to be interested in local politics, know about candidates, be mobilized, and report that issues influenced their vote choice. Even more noteworthy is that, among these factors, the most glaring differences are between homeowners and renters. Homeowners are twice as likely to report knowing a lot about council candidates, more than 50 percent more likely to personally know a candidate, and were nearly 20 percent more likely to say their vote was based on a particular issue. Given that this sample already selects among a highly engaged segment of the population, these differences are quite stark. As noted in chapter 2, the most attentive participants in local politics continue to be homeowners.

The other notable differences occur along racial lines. With a few exceptions, whites in the SSV sample exhibit higher levels of political engagement than minorities. Although both blacks and whites report similar levels of political interest, whites were nearly twice as likely to report knowing a lot about candidates, were about half as more likely to personally know candidates, and were about 9

TABLE 5.2
Differences in Political Interest, Mobilization, and Information by Individual Education, Race, Homeownership, and Length of Residence

	Very or Somewhat Interested in Local Politics	Know a Lot or a Fair Amount about City Council Candidates	Know a Council Canidate Personally	Were Contacted by Local Organizations	Agree that Local Issues Influenced Vote Choice
Education (in years)					
0–12 years	75	44	28	42	92
12-16 years	76	45	31	51	89
13 or more years	65	51	37	59	89
Homeownership					
No	64	28	22	38	74
Yes	78	50	36	52	91
Live 10 years in town?					
No	72	35	27	48	89
Yes	78	52	38	52	90
Race					
White (n = 1007)	76	50	33	52	90
Black (n = 108)	76	28	23	43	92
Hispanic (n = 35)	65	34	25	56	83
Asian (n = 16)	66	29	7	44	100

Source: The 2004–2005 Study of the Suburban Voter (SSV).

Note: Numbers in the table are percentages; the total number of cases is 1,166.

percent more likely to be mobilized to vote. Nearly similar differences also exist between whites and Latinos and Asian Americans, although the small numbers of these latter groups in the sample inhibit our ability to draw any strong conclusions from these numbers. These racial differences are all the more striking considering that the places in the SSV sample include a large number of towns with significant minority populations and that the SSV is already sampling from an engaged portion of the citizenry. Although the issue of minority representation will be taken up in greater detail in chapter 6, these findings show that minorities may be more marginalized in smaller places than they are in large cities.

But while these cross-tabulations are quite suggestive, it is impossible to draw any definitive conclusions from them or to compare the magnitude of differences across factors. In other words, we cannot tell from these simple statistics how much the differences between renters and homeowners may be attributable to their individual level of education, their race, or the types of communities they live in. In order to examine the relative effects of both the contextual and individual-level variables, a multivariate analysis is required, and, given the small number of places all the voters come from, a set of hierarchical linear models (HLM) are the most appropriate estimation procedure. The results are listed in table 5.3.

Even when the individual-level characteristics and other demographic characteristics of the municipalities are taken into account, the patterns illustrated in the cross-tabulations remain. As in the cross-tabulations, community size remains one of the most important determinants of local political engagement. Voters in larger places are, on average, less interested in politics, less knowledgeable of city council candidates, and are less likely to be mobilized during the campaign. The multivariate analyses suggest that people in more racially heterogeneous places are more interested in local politics. Furthermore, the institutional structure of the town makes a difference: voters in places with mayoral elections are more interested in local politics, more likely to know a city council candidate personally, and more likely to be mobilized; voters in affluent places and places with partisan elections are more likely to be mobilized; and voters in places with off-cycle elections are more likely to reference particular issues that shape their vote choice.

At the individual level, the biggest factors relating to voters' local political engagement were homeownership, length of residence, education, and race. As in the cross-tabulations and the findings from chapter 2, homeowners exhibited greater interest in politics, more knowledge of local candidates, higher mobilization rates, and were more animated by local issues. Given that the models controlled for length of residence in the community (which is also positively related to political interest and knowledge of candidates), the effects of homeownership seem even more impressive. Education is also correlated with political knowledge,

TABLE 5.3
Multi-Level Model Results of Suburban Electoral Culture

		Interest in Local Campaigns (1= Completely Uninterested 4 = Very Interested)	Mean Knowledge of City Council Candidates (1= Never Heard of 5 = Know a Lot)	Personal Acquaintance of a Local Council Candidate	Contacted by Local Organizations	Vote Choice Influenced by Local Issues
Intercept	Intercept	2.64**	1.87**	−1.43**	−.74*	.14
(β_{0j})	(γ_{00})	(.12)	(.10)	(.38)	(.27)	(.25)
	IQV	.37^	.30	.77	.13	−.40
	(γ_{01})	(.19)	(.25)	(.57)	(.63)	(.55)
	Population	−.14**	−.25**	−.76**	−.25	.12
	(γ_{02})	(.04)	(.05)	(.12)	(.15)	(.18)
	MHI	.09	.22	.46	.59*	−.14
	(γ_{03})	(.15)	(.13)	(.40)	(.25)	(.28)
	Partisan Elec.	.01	−.11	−.17	.52^-	−.11
	(γ_{04})	(.10)	(.12)	(.26)	(.25)	(.29)
	Mayoral Elec.	.33**	.02	.67*	.92**	−.12
	(γ_{05})	(.09)	(.12)	(.24)	(.25)	(.35)
	Off-Cycle Elec.	−.04	−.16	−.06	−.27	.78^
	(γ_{06})	(.12)	(.12)	(.28)	(.31)	(.41)
Education	Intercept	.01	.07**	.01	.16**	.09^
(β_{1j})	(γ_{10})	(.02)	(.02)	(.05)	(.06)	(.05)
Own Home	Intercept	.23**	.40**	.57^	.48**	.88**
(β_{2j})	(γ_{20})	(.08)	(.06)	(.31)	(.16)	(.21)
Live +10	Intercept	.13*	.25**	.49**	.16	.05
Yrs (β_{3j})	(γ_{30})	(.05)	(.04)	(.16)	(.13)	(.16)
Female	Intercept	.07	−.01	−.01	.21^	−.29*
(β_{4j})	(γ_{40})	(.06)	(.05)	(.13)	(.12)	(.12)
Age	Intercept.	.01	.01	−.01	−.01	−.01**
(β_{5j})	(γ_{50})	(.01)	(.01)	(.01)	(.01)	(.004)
Black+	Intercept	−.07	−.31**	−.79**	−.51*	.10
(β_{6j})	(γ_{60})	(.12)	(.08)	(.28)	(.21)	(.26)
Latino+	Intercept	−.71	.29*	−.50^	.47	−.03
(β_{7j})	(γ_{70})	(.13)	(.11)	(.29)	(.22)	(.32)
Asian+	Intercept	−.35**	−.43**	-2.35*	.51	−.73^
(β_{8j})	(γ_{80})	(.11)	(.11)	(.95)	(.34)	(.38)
Other	Intercept	.08	−.13	.14	−.07	.17
Race+	(γ_{90})	(.10)	(.10)	(.32)	(.22)	(.21)
(β_{9j})						
N (level-1)		1,371	1,374	1,241	1,359	1,378

Source: The 2004–2005 Study of the Suburban Voter (SSV).

Note: All variables at the level 1 are centered around their group means, except for dummy variables. All variables at the level 2 are grand-centered. The results from the unit-specific models are reported in the case of Bernoulli model. Robust standard errors are in parentheses.

** $p < .01$;   * $p < .05$;   ^ $p < .1$ (two-tailed)

+ "White" used as a baseline category

mobilization, and attention to local issues, which is unsurprisingly consistent with previous studies on voting behavior (Verba, Schlozman, and Brady 1995; Wolfinger and Rosenstone 1980). Interestingly, racial minorities in general were less knowledgeable about candidates, while Asian Americans were less interested in local campaigns and African Americans were less mobilized during local elections, although Hispanics in the sample were more likely to be mobilized.

In sum, these findings suggest that among local voters there is a very high level of political engagement, although it varies somewhat in relation to the size and scope of a municipality, even after controlling for several individual-level factors like age and education. Even though larger places presumably have more community issues before them, their bigger population size corresponds with less voter interest and knowledge about local campaigns. In places with greater scope (as indicated by having a popularly elected mayor), voters report being more engaged by local politics. Local electoral politics also vary in relation to a voter's individual status in the community. Stakeholders in the community (i.e., older, educated homeowners, and long-term residents) are more engaged by local affairs, familiar with candidates, and mobilized in local politics. Thus not only are these stakeholders already more likely to vote in the first place but, even among voters, they are also even more engaged, informed, and connected to the political life of their communities. The SSV data also reveal a racial bias to local political engagement—minorities are generally less connected with local candidates and are less likely to be recruited by local campaigns. Even in racially mixed places, as the ones we sampled from, electoral politics is circumscribed by race.

How Much Are Local Voters like National Voters?

So how does the political engagement of these local voters translate into actual voting behavior? As with the aggregate studies of voting behavior in chapter 4, the answer to this question hinges on our ability to develop a comparable metric across all different elections. And, as in chapter 4, this metric can be found in support for incumbents. To review the rationale for this metric, remember that incumbency is perhaps the most important factor shaping people's ballot decisions. Incumbent candidates have numerous benefits of office, including opportunities to enhance their name recognition, to perform various acts of retail politics, and to link with various constituencies, and, by one estimate, they are overwhelmingly favored by local newspapers (Ansolabehere, Lessem, and Snyder. 2006). Not surprisingly, they also do a good job at getting reelected. In the municipalities of the SSV sample, 47 of 56 incumbents running for reelection in city council elections were returned to office, as were 10 of the 11 mayoral incumbents. As noted in chapter 4, given the limited scope of most local governments, it is reasonable to assume that local elections are, first and foremost, referenda on incumbent performance (Zaller 2004).

But if supporting incumbents is the default voting position of people in low-information contexts, then the central question for explaining electoral behavior is what drives local voters to deviate from this trend and vote for challengers? Is it because of some general dissatisfaction with the way the municipality is being governed? Does it reflect a particular concern with local economic conditions? Or, do other determinants of vote choice, such as partisanship, community issues, or candidate likeability come into play?

To answer these questions, let us examine city council races in the SSV sample where at least one incumbent was running in a contested election and where all the elections were for at-large seats.[3] The primary variable of interest is a scale of incumbency support. Since voters had opportunities to vote for numerous candidates in the city council elections, voters were placed in one of three groups: (1) those supporting only incumbents, (2) those supporting some incumbents and some challengers, and (3) those supporting only challengers.[4] As predictors of incumbency support, let us look at

[3] By doing so, we lose three cities, Oak Brook, Oak Park, and Pittsburg, where no incumbent ran for reelection.

[4] When constructing vote choice variables, we exclude all invalid votes, which mean that a respondent reported casting more than the number of votes allowed in the city council

several different measures that gauge voters' perceptions of the candidates, including their appraisal of candidate likeability, their issue agreement with the candidates, their personal acquaintance with the candidate, and if they shared partisanship with the candidate.[5] Given the importance of retrospective evaluations of incumbents, let us also compare these groups of voters by the subjective impression they had of local economic conditions and government performance.[6] The bottom of table 5.4 lists cross-tabulations for all three groups of voters across all of these variables.

The most striking finding from the cross-tabulations is the importance of issues relative to either candidate partisanship or personal characteristics. As expected, candidate likeability, issue agreement, and shared partisanship all correspond with voting patterns—the more a voter liked or agreed with challengers or incumbents, the more likely he or she voted for challengers or incumbents respectively—their relative effects, however, differ. Whereas national elections typically hinge on partisan affiliations and subjective appraisals of candidate likeability, in local elections, the candidates' issue positions seem to be the most important correlate of voter support. Much of this is simply related to the fact that over half the sample cannot identify the party of the candidates or does not have a personal assessment of the candidates. Once

election: for instance, if a respondent reported voting for three city council candidates when only two seats were open, then his or her vote is considered invalid. Also, the votes of the respondents whose number of votes in city council elections is zero are considered invalid. The percentage of valid votes in city council elections ranges from 42 (Hazel Crest) to 86 (Milpitas and Solana Beach).

[5] Given that voters in city council races had a choice of numerous incumbents and that most voters had numerous choices among challengers, we constructed four three-point ordinal variables relative to incumbent support. Taking candidate likeability, for example, -1 denotes that the number of incumbents a respondent liked was greater than that of challengers, 0 denotes that the number of incumbents he or she liked was equal to that of challengers, and 1 indicates that the number of incumbents he or she liked was smaller than that of challengers.

[6] SSV respondents were asked about their impression of local economic conditions over the past year: whether it had gotten better, stayed the same or gotten worse. Respondents were also asked how well they thought that "local government in [their community] is working": very well, somewhat well, somewhat badly, or very badly. For the later measure, the variable was recoded into two categories.

TABLE 5.4
Key Determinants of City Council Vote Choice

	Vote for Incumbents Only (n = 317)	Vote for Both Challengers and Incumbents (n = 323)	Vote for Challengers Only (n = 217)
Likeability (n = 857)			
Prefer Incumbents	51	17	2
Like Both	16	53	18
Prefer Challengers	1	9	47
No Response	32	21	34
Issue Agreement (n = 857)			
Agree w/ Incumbents	66	10	0
Agree w/ Both	13	76	15
Agree w/ Challengers	1	6	66
No Response	20	8	19
Personal Acquaintance (n = 857)			
Know Incumbents	26	16	3
Know Both	4	24	10
Know Challengers	0	11	21
No Response	70	49	66
Shared Partisanship (n = 857)			
Share w/ Incumbents	35	7	3
Share w/ Both	6	25	6
Share w/ Challengers	2	7	33
No Response	57	61	58
Mean Familiarity Score with Challengers (n = 855)			
1 = Never heard of; 5 = Know a lot	3.1	2.6	3.7
Perceptions on City Economy* (n = 813)			
Worse	31	39	30
Same/Better	39	39	22
Perceptions on Local Government Performance* (n = 832)			
Good	39	39	22
Bad	25	33	41

Source: The 2004–2005 Study of the Suburban Voter (SSV).

Note: Numbers in the table are percentages.

* Row percentage = 100

again, this is probably due to the nonpartisan character of many of these local elections and the difficulty that candidates have in making themselves known to voters. When candidates are so unknown as people and when their partisanship is either a mystery or irrelevant, then the crucial determinants of presidential voting no longer hold.

What emerges instead are issues and retrospective voting. Far and away, the most common correlate of voting support was issue congruence with a candidate. Not only did 4 out 5 voters report sharing an issue position with a candidate, but this issue position was in strong congruence with their vote choice. Voters who agreed with only incumbents on issues tended to vote for more incumbents than challengers and vice-versa. While this fact may seem self-evident, it is important to compare it in relationship to other characteristics. Remember, local voters are far less likely to report sharing partisanship with candidates or making personal evaluations of them than sharing views on issues. The fact that issue congruence is so much higher than these other traits suggests that local voters base their voting decisions first and foremost on the policy stances and past behaviors of the candidates.

Similarly, evaluations of local economic conditions or government performance also correspond with incumbent support. Not surprisingly, people who think their local economy is doing well or that their local government is doing a good job are also more likely to support incumbents. The magnitude of these retrospective evaluations, however, is small because, unlike in national politics, most local voters seem pretty happy with their communities. In the SSV sample, 76 percent of the respondents thought their city economy had done the same or better in the past year, and about 80 percent thought that local government performance was good. Although such contentment may be a function of the higher social status of voters compared to nonvoters, it nevertheless shows that local *voters* are a generally satisfied lot. This would also suggest why incumbents tend to do well in elections. If most voters think their towns are well managed, then it is hardly surprising they would support the governing regime.

Once again, it is impossible to know to what extent these simple statistics are a function of unmeasured individual or place-specific characteristics, such as population size, income, or race. Thus, in order to take these various influences into account, let us return to multivariate analysis using a hierarchical generalized linear model predicting support for challengers. The dependent variable is a three-point scale of challenger support (1 = incumbents only; 3 = challengers only). For explanatory variables, the baseline model (Model 1) includes the three-point measures of likeability, issue agreement, and shared partisanship in conjunction with a five-point scale variable of candidate familiarity, and several other individual-level measures, including perceptions of the city economy, local government performance, homeownership, length of residency, interest in local campaigns, mobilization, education, age and gender. Measures of size, scope (whether the election was off-cycle and the town had a mayor), and bias (measured once again with partisan elections, median household income, and a measure of racial diversity) are also added. The results are presented in table 5.5.

The more sophisticated, multivariate models suggest that, as in the cross-tabulations, sharing issue positions with the candidates is the strongest predictor of local voting behavior. Although voters who thought that challengers were either more likeable, shared their party affiliations, or shared their issue stances were also much more likely to vote for challengers, the shared issue positions exhibit the strongest relationship to support for challengers: compared to voters who preferred incumbents, voters who were personally drawn to just challengers were, according to our estimates, only 15 percent more likely to vote for just challengers, and those who shared partisanship with challengers were 19 percent more likely to vote for just challengers; meanwhile, those who agreed with challengers on issues were 45 percent more likely to vote for just challengers.[7] Voters were also more likely to support

---

[7] These predicted probabilities are calculated from ordered probit models estimated in Stata, using CLARIFY software (King, Tomz, and Wittenberg 2000; Tomz, Wittenberg, and

TABLE 5.5
Vote Choice for Challengers in City Council Elections

		Model 1	Model 2	Model 3	Model 4
Intercept	Intercept	−2.13**	−2.33**	−2.18**	−1.95**
(β_{0j})	(γ_{00})	(.49)	(.48)	(.49)	(.39)
	IQV	2.05^	1.98	3.04	2.15
	(γ_{01})	(1.08)	(1.09)	(1.11)	(1.08)
	Population	−.60**	−.61**	−.76**	−.60**
	(γ_{02})	(.20)	(.20)	(.24)	(.20)
	MHI	−.08	−.12	−.08	−.08
	(γ_{03})	(.77)	(.78)	(.80)	(.77)
	Partisan Elec.	.37	.38	.33	.39
	(γ_{04})	(.50)	(.51)	(.51)	(.52)
	Mayoral Elec.	.94^	.95^	.83	.92^
	(γ_{05})	(.47)	(.47)	(.46)	(.48)
	Off-Cycle Elec.	−.01	−.01	.13	.01
	(γ_{06})	(.66)	(.67)	(.67)	(.67)
Likeability	Intercept	.54**	.53**	.55**	.55**
(β_{1j})	(γ_{10})	(.11)	(.12)	(.12)	(.11)
Issue Agreement	Intercept	1.66**	1.73**	1.70**	1.66**
(β_{2j})	(γ_{20})	(.16)	(.17)	(.16)	(.16)
	Population		.39*		
	(γ_{21})		(.16)		
	IQV		.59		
	(γ_{22})		(.60)		
Shared Partisanship	Intercept	.88**	.89**	.86**	.84**
(β_{3j})	(γ_{30})	(.18)	(.19)	(.18)	(.16)
	Partisan Election				.84*
	(γ_{31})				(.37)
Familiarity	Intercept	.30*	.31**	.29*	.30*
(β_{4j})	(γ_{40})	(.12)	(.12)	(.12)	(.12)

challengers if they were more interested in local campaigns: voters who reported being very interested in the local campaigns were 10 percent more likely to vote for only challengers than those who were completely uninterested in the campaigns. The multilevel analyses confirm a finding from cross-tabulations that voters who

King 2003). The probit models used the same set of variables as the HLM models, although the coefficients do not take into account the biases arising from a limited set of contexts. Nevertheless, they provide a convenient way of generating some predicted probabilities.

TABLE 5.5 (cont'd)
Vote Choice for Challengers in City Council Elections

		Model 1	Model 2	Model 3	Model 4
Perception on City Economy; Positive (β_{5j})	Intercept (γ_{50})	.07 (.10)	.02 (.10)	.06 (.10)	.06 (.09)
Local Gov't Performance; Positive (β_{6j})	Intercept (γ_{60})	−.52** (.18)	−.45* (.19)	−.54** (.17)	−.52** (.40)
Education (β_{7j})	Intercept (γ_{70})	.12^ (.07)	.13^ (.07)	.11 (.07)	.11 (.07)
Own Home (β_{8j})	Intercept (γ_{80})	.24 (.26)	.32 (.24)	.29 (.26)	.24 (.26)
Live + 10 Yrs. (β_{9j})	Intercept (γ_{90})	−.20 (.18)	−.20 (.18)	−.21 (.18)	−.24 (.17)
Interest (β_{10j})	Intercept (γ_{100})	.40** (.14)	.39** (.14)	.37** (.14)	.41** (.14)
Mobilization (β_{11j})	Intercept (γ_{110})	.33^ (.20)	.39* (.20)	.33* (.15)	.31 (.20)
	Population (γ_{111})			.44** (.16)	
	IQV (γ_{112})		(.66)	−1.95	
Female (β_{12j})	Intercept (γ_{120})	.17 (.17)	.17 (.18)	.17 (.16)	.17 (.17)
Age (β_{13j})	Intercept (γ_{130})	−.01 (.01)	−.01 (.01)	−.01 (.01)	−.01 (.01)

Source: The 2004–2005 Study of the Suburban Voter (SSV).

Note: All variables at the level 1 are centered around their group means, except for dummy variables. All variables at the level 2 are grand-centered. Robust standard errors are in parentheses. The number of cases is 738.

** p < .01; * p < .05; ^ p < .1 (two-tailed)

have negative perceptions of local government performance were more likely to vote for challengers, although evaluations of economic conditions had no impact.

Support for challengers was also related to the size, scope, and bias of a community. In contrast with the aggregate findings in chapter 4, among the SSV sample, challengers got less support in larger places than in smaller ones. If the coefficients are translated into probabilities, voters in the smallest places were 19 percent more likely to support only challengers compared to voters in the largest places. Many of these differences are related to the different levels of political engagement between voters in small and larger places. As we saw earlier, people in smaller places are more involved in local politics, more informed about local issues, and more familiar with candidates. Given their greater engagement, they are probably more likely to know about challengers or be animated by specific issues.

Indeed, this is what the data suggest. Additional multilevel models were run with interaction terms between two key individual variables (shared issue positions and mobilization) and population size. Model 2 shows the results from the interaction between population size and issue positions. According to this equation, issues work to counterbalance the impact of population size. In other words, the greater level of challenger support among voters in smaller places is largely attributable to the ability of voters to link them to particular issues. Once this issue connection is specifically taken into account, the effects of population size diminish. A similar pattern also works with voter mobilization (as seen in Model 3). Mobilization also offsets the negative effects of challenger support by population size. In other words, once the different mobilization levels of the campaigns are taken into account, the differences in incumbent support between larger and smaller places diminish. Mobilization also occurs around partisanship (as illustrated in Model 4) and partisan affiliation with a candidate is far more important in places with partisan elections than nonpartisan elections.

Together, these findings begin to provide some clues about the differences in campaign and election dynamics between smaller and larger places. In larger places, challenger support partly hinges on the ability of candidates to link themselves to voters around salient issues. Presumably then, in larger communities different groups are contesting key policies of local government, forming candidacies around these issues, and promoting these issue positions to the voters at large. Yet incumbents are not taking these challenges lying down. Rather, in places where challengers might have more advantages, incumbents who attract more votes are those who are mobilizing supporters more actively, either directly or through partisan appeals. In short, the social and political terrain of the suburb affects the nature of campaign dynamics that, in turn, shape the pattern of vote choice.

The biggest surprise in the multivariate models is the absence of individual-level demographic traits as a predictor of vote choice. Although homeowners, the educated, and long-term residents were more interested in local affairs and more knowledgeable about candidates, and thus presumably more likely to be supportive of challengers, there were no significant differences in the challenger support scale along any of these dimensions (except for education). Nor were there any significant differences in incumbency support between voters in off-cycle versus concurrent elections, which is probably the result of the sampling screens (respondents were taken only if they said they voted in local elections) and voter roll-off (only those interested in local elections continued voting past the national ticket; see Wattenberg, McAllister, and Salvanto 2000).[8] Either way, whatever differences that occur between homeowners and renters, short- and long-term residents, or voters seem to be subsumed by other individual-level factors such as candidate issue positions or subjective evaluations of candidates. These differences reinforce the importance of the distinct character of the local voter: when only the most informed and interested portion of the electorate casts a ballot, the determinants of vote choice tend to be focused more on specific issues and less on heuristics like partisanship or candidate likeability.

CONCLUSION

From the data in this chapter, we are left with a surprising and paradoxical conclusion: your average voter in a local election is far more interested, engaged, and informed about local politics than the average voter in a presidential election. To the reader who skipped to the conclusion of this chapter, such an assertion may seem ridiculous. After all, presidential elections are the subjects of intense public scrutiny. They receive massive amounts

[8] In the SSV sample, the proportion of the respondents who participated in the November 2004 presidential election, but did not cast valid votes in the local council election, was 27 percent. Among those who did not vote in local elections, 48 percent reported that they were "somewhat" or "very" interested in local campaigns, which is significantly smaller than the 77.7 percent who cast votes in both presidential and local election.

of media coverage and the campaign organizers spend hundreds of millions of dollars promoting their candidates. Most voters in presidential elections also have clear and strong preferences about whom they will support long before the first Tuesday in November. Meanwhile, local elections happen at odd times, often get little or no media coverage, are often uncontested, and rarely hinge on the chronic ideological divisions that appear to characterize national politics.

Yet, despite these tremendous differences in media exposure, most voters in national elections know relatively little about the candidates beyond their faces, party affiliation, and maybe their stance on a few issues that are largely in line with their party platforms (Bartels 1996). Meanwhile, voters in most local elections, at least as represented in the SSV data, appear to be quite knowledgeable about candidates, exhibit interest in local politics, and focus more on candidates' issue positions than on factors like party, charisma, or even personal acquaintance. Given these differences in publicity between national and local elections, why would local voters appear to be so much better informed than national ones?

This paradox is largely due to the selective differences in voter turnout between national and local elections and their symbolic meaning. When 60 to 70 percent of eligible citizens turnout to vote, as occurs in most national contests (Popkin 2004), the electorate will inevitably include a significant portion of citizens for whom politics is a secondary concern at best. This is partly because national elections are arguably the most important collective ritual that unites all citizens of the United States. Voting for the president is one of the few activities that all adult citizens share in common and that gets performed on the same day. In the same way that churches are filled with the less devout or doctrinally ignorant on Easter and Christmas, so presidential elections will include citizens whose average education, interest in politics, or information about public affairs is likely to be relatively low.

Local elections, because they often occur at odd times and with less-known candidates, ironically attract a much different type of voter: one who is not only a stakeholder in his or her community, but is also quite interested in local affairs, knowledgeable about local candidates, and focused on particular issues surrounding the community. When only 20 percent of citizens vote, and when these tend to be the most educated and established residents of a community, then their average level of local knowledge is likely to be much higher. Furthermore, local elections do not have the same kind of existential meaning as national contests. For voters in places like Riverdale, Muttontown, or Daly City, it is unlikely that their town residence provides anywhere near the same kind of meaningful social identity that their American citizenship does and the ritual of going to the polling place in April is unlikely to have the same amount of social significance that voting in November does. This makes a tremendous difference in the type of person who is making a voting decision. To return to the earlier metaphor, if your average national voter is like someone who attends church only on Easter, your average local voter is someone who is likely to be found in services on a cold, grey February morning and can probably cite entire passages of scripture from memory.

Given these differences in information and engagement, it should be hardly surprising that local voters also use somewhat different criteria in making their electoral decisions than their national counterparts. Partisanship and candidate charisma are so important in national elections because the average voter knows so little about national politics. In the absence of any clear understanding about what the candidates stand for, party and personality become important heuristics for voters to match their preferences with the candidates, albeit with a relatively low level of accuracy (Bartels 1996). In other words, because Barack Obama is a Democrat and seems like a very measured and pragmatic leader, most voters could probably make a good guess about where he is likely to stand on any range of issues from gun control to support for free trade.

Partisanship and candidate charisma are less important in local elections not just because elections are nonpartisan or because citizens have so much less exposure to their local leaders, but ironically because the information levels of the average voter are so much higher. When elections include only the civic elite, then votes will be based less on heuristics or other information shortcuts, and more on specific issues. The civically engaged citizen is far more likely to be an "issue voter" precisely because he or she is so much more attentive to the concerns of the community.

Because the issue concerns of localities are so parochial and seemingly insignificant to outsiders, we may be excused for dismissing them as a significant factor in voting behavior. For example, the fact that a few residents of West Windsor, New Jersey are in an uproar over a parking lot expansion or that people in Malibu are bitterly divided over a proposed shopping mall, may seem not only trivial but also ridiculous to all other Americans. But just because the local concerns of any one community are specific to that place, it does not lessen their importance as a factor in local elections. Indeed, issues are so crucial to local elections precisely because they are so parochial. In a managerial democracy, issues are the only factors that will divide a population in the absence of gross corruption, malfeasance, or fiscal mismanagement.

This brings us back to the example of the "Iceman." Voting for the Jerry Butler simply because of his nickname is not that unusual. This is not only because voters use heuristics to determine who they should support, but because Jerry Butler was running in what could be called a nonlocal election (i.e., he is running for a commission seat in a county of over 3 million people). If people vote for the "Iceman" because of his nickname, they are behaving like typical voters in national and state elections—they are making choices based on pretty flimsy criteria. Local voters tend to be more informed than this. Although they may not always know all the candidates or their policy positions, they tend to be much better informed about these matters than voters in state or national elections. If Jerry Butler were running for mayor of Riverdale or a council position in Oak Park, he probably would not need to put his nickname on the ballot, because he would be personally known by many of his constituents and most would know him based on his performance and stances on pass issues. If this were the case, the "Iceman" part of his identity would probably melt away

CHAPTER 6

Rethinking Local Democracy

ON THE EVENING of November 4, 2008, America putatively held its breath as it awaited the results of the presidential election. The major news networks offered a dramatic spin to the otherwise banal exercise of tabulating results, with state-of-the-art computer technology, scores of political experts offering up-to-the-minute commentary, maps and charts of all sizes and colors, and, in the case of CNN, even a holographic image of one of its reporters. Yet, for all the theatrics, the outcome of this election was already well known. As early as August, over two months before the election and even when John McCain was ahead in the polls, political scientists offered forecasts of an Obama victory that were remarkably close to the actual results. So while the networks were fueling America's collective suspense, the outcome was a foregone conclusion, at least to experts on voting behavior.

The irony was that while the networks were handwringing over an election whose results were foretold, they paid almost no attention to most of the races whose outcomes were actually unclear. Among the thousands of local elections that were also taking place on November 4, there were hundreds for which no prognostications could be made and whose outcomes were truly suspenseful. Although the discrepancy in media coverage is understandable (after all, why should people in Georgia care about local elections in Montana?), the discrepancy in our predictive capacity between the two types of different elections is more surprising. If we can predict how most Americans are going to vote for president months before an election, then why can't we predict who is likely to win in the average American city's election for mayor or city council?

The answer is partly to be found in our perspective: because we tend to look at all elections as categorically similar, our default expectation is that the same factors that drive presidential elections will shape local ones. But clearly elections for a suburban city council seat are very different than that of the president, and until we find a way to differentiate national, state, and local democracies from each other, we cannot differentiate their electoral politics. As I've argued throughout this book, identifying the size, scope, and bias provides just such a framework for doing this.

Consider the forecasts of presidential elections. As with any democracies that are large in size, great in scope, and high in bias, American presidential elections are predictable precisely because they are defined by long-standing political cleavages: with its great size, the United States holds innumerable groups of people with different interests and identities; with its great scope, it evokes sharp ideological divisions over the ideal relationship between society and the state; and with its high bias, it contains large numbers of special interest groups with a particular stake in a variety of government programs. Candidates, parties, interest groups, and other political actors coalesce around these durable political fault lines and organize their electoral efforts accordingly. For instance, national campaigns know that a certain percentage of Americans identify with one party or another and work to mobilize their own partisans, and they also know that some states are solidly "red" or "blue" and probably not worth contesting. It is this enduring level of political conflict that makes the outcome of the election relatively easy to predict.[1]

The same is not the case with most local or small-scale elections. Because most American localities are socially homogeneous, have a narrow scope, and are relatively unbiased, they have few of the permanent political divisions that exist on the nation or state level. They are managerial democracies. This makes the outcome of local elections both easier and more difficult to predict.

---

[1] In fact, the models that accurately predict presidential elections are remarkably simple in the number of variables they employ.

On the one hand, in managerial democracies, most incumbents run unopposed or win reelection when they do face an opponent. Much of this is attributable to the absence of a highly motivated and well-organized opposition perpetually contesting their seats. Most localities are simply too small, weak, and unbiased to sustain long-standing political cleavages that characterize politics in larger democracies. When strong opposition groups do arise in local politics, they tend to be motivated by specific issues that are both parochial and temporal.

On the other hand, the absence of chronic political cleavages in most localities also means that it is very difficult to predict when a certain issue, event, or personality is likely to animate an otherwise dormant constituency and motivate voters to select someone new. It is very hard to foretell when a problematic issue becomes incendiary, it is unclear what makes a quality opponent suddenly decide to run for an office with little power or pay, and, as any politician can attest, it is impossible to foresee when some random comment mushrooms into a major political controversy. Ironically, the unpredictability of local politics also is exacerbated by the selective nature of the local electorate. Because "homevoters" are so attuned to local affairs and so personally connected to local politics, they are that much easier to mobilize around a specific issue. Local politics in managerial democracy may be mostly tranquil, but local voters are far from docile, and it is difficult to anticipate when or why they will strike.

Of course, this description of local elections is not universal to all small places in America. Even the smallest and most unbiased managerial democracy will occasionally have political divisions that fester over longer periods of time. Hard feelings over a minor political squabble may persist for years, particularly among those at the losing end of a political controversy. And because the actors in the local political drama are likely to know each other firsthand and run into each other as neighbors, the flames of resentment may continue to be stoked. There are also places where rapid demographic changes put long-standing political regimes at odds with their constituencies, such as among places with dramatic racial turnout, as we saw with Zenovia Evans in Riverdale, or with a generational cohort that holds different partisan allegiances, as we saw with Tom Jester in Deerfield, Illinois. In short, the predictions about the political impact of size, scope, and bias are not unbreakable laws and exceptions may occur.

This characterization of local politics in a managerial democracy may come as a surprise to many readers. It certainly stands in contrast to most of what is written about American electoral politics in general and about local politics in particular. What remains unclear is what all of this means for local democracy in America. Does the managerial character of most American democracies favor certain groups above others? Does managerial democracy inhibit or enhance the capacity of most Americans for meaningful self-governance? Who governs in a managerial democracy?

This concluding chapter offers some answers. As with other aspects of local politics, the key to understanding the democratic implications of local governance is to be found by first differentiating local democracies by their size, scope, and bias. Because most American municipalities are relatively small in size, scope, and bias, most of our existing theories and studies about local politics and civic participation are inappropriate. Most of what we think about local democracy is informed by a handful of studies of big cities, yet big cities are fundamentally different from the types of places where most Americans live. Once we consider the smaller size and lower scope and bias of most American places, our way of understanding local democracy changes. In most places, local democracy is less about coalitions of property speculators and machine politicians establishing local fiefdoms or about marginalized groups, such as minorities or the poor, empowering themselves through civic activism. Rather, it is more about large portions of the electorate attaining relatively easy consensus over the general management of a limited number of government services and a greater stratification of different groups across municipal boundaries. Local democracy in suburban America is less about intramunicipal political struggle than it is about intermunicipal political exclusion. This situation creates a much more complicated picture of "who governs" America than what most existing research suggests.

ON LOCAL POLITICAL POWER

In chapter 1, we noted that most political observers tend to view all elections as categorically similar phenomena and that most of their expectations about voter behavior are based on studies of presidential contests. The same could be said for our understanding of local politics. When political observers think about local politics they usually draw on the rich literature about big cities, which tends to fall into two camps: one group is focused primarily on urban political coalitions whose members are differentiated by their views of economic development, patronage, and race; the other group is focused on the putative benefits of local civic participation, particularly for empowering otherwise marginal groups. Because these studies comprise nearly all the research on local politics, they have almost singularly defined how political scientists think about local democracy and governance. Yet, from the perspective outlined earlier in this book, their insights may not necessarily apply to the vast majority of places where most Americans live. When considering the size, scope, and bias of all American places, the dominant models of local politics are germane to only a small portion of American localities or at least certain political circumstances. This means it may be time to rethink local politics, or at least to differentiate it from urban politics or theories of civic participation.

To appreciate this point, a very brief overview of the scholarly perspective on local politics is in order. When political scientists discuss local politics in America, they usually start with a debate initiated in the 1950s over the nature of "community power." On one side were sociologists like C. Wright Mills (1956) and Floyd Hunter (1953) who claimed that local politics was the politics of elite domination. Looking at politics in Atlanta, for example, Hunter found the most decisive authors of public policy tended to be a small number of senior executives from the biggest corporations in the city. This select group not only headed the largest businesses, but also sat on the boards of the biggest nonprofits, and tended to have direct access to elected officials and their policy decisions. Mills saw this elite domination as an inevitable consequence of a society dominated by large, highly specialized, and hierarchical organizations like multinational corporations, government agencies, and universities that effectively channeled decision-making into a few hands.

On the other side of the debate were political scientists like Robert Dahl (1961), Nelson Polsby (1980), and Ray Wolfinger (1974) who argued that the sources of interest and power in urban governance were more pluralistic and varied in relationship to specific policy areas. In their multiple studies of New Haven, Connecticut, they observed that local business leaders were interested in some policies (e.g., urban redevelopment) but not others (e.g., municipal hiring or education). Big cities had multiple sources of political power such as with ethnic and racial groups seeking greater political incorporation (Browning, Marshall, and Tabb 2003) or political machines and other types of patronage networks (Banfield and Wilson 1963). The "pluralists" argued that this multiplicity of preferences created a heterogeneous and often cacophonous realm of governance that defied easy characterization.

By the 1980s, scholars began synthesizing these competing views and refining their earlier concepts. The first major contribution came from political scientist Paul Peterson (1981), who observed that a municipality's political agenda is fundamentally constrained by its geographic limitations and the American system of federalism. Peterson deduced that because localities cannot control the flows of labor or capital out of their jurisdictions, they must focus primarily on issues related to land and adjust their policies to find the balance between the tax rates their constituents will tolerate and the policies they demand. In contrast with neo-Marxist accounts, Peterson observed that the competition among localities and states for tax "ratables" (those constituents who pay more in taxes than get in services) would dramatically limit the capacity of any locality to significantly redistribute capital. Because of this, localities would tend to focus on "developmental" policies that seek to lay the groundwork for further economic growth or "allocational" policies that will benefit all residents uniformly.[2]

The second contribution came from sociologists John Logan and Harvey Molotch (1987) and political scientist John Mollenkopf (1983), who extended Peterson's insights about the land-centered orientation of local politics to identify the motivations of key political actors. If property issues are at the heart of local politics, then patterns of political activity will be defined by the relationships of various constituencies to the land. Property holders who seek profits (or "exchange value") from their real estate investments have quantifiable motivations for shaping local politics compared to renters or small land-holders who seek only "use value" from property and whose interest in local politics are more difficult to specify. Given this discrepancy, these analysts surmise that urban politics are dominated by a "growth machine" unified in its concern to maximize commercial property values. This machine includes not just business elites who work in areas of commercial property, such as bankers, real estate developers, and insurance brokers, but also the locally elected officials who come from their ranks, large local nonprofits like museums and universities, local media outlets like newspapers and television stations, and any other major institutions with significant investments in a particular place. Using policies like selective zoning, infrastructure improvements, and tax variances to improve the value of commercial property investments, Logan and Molotch persuasively argued that this "growth machine" will be a dominant political force in most large cities.

The third major contribution came from political scientists Stephen Elkin (1987) and Clarence Stone (1989), who observed the conditions under which a "growth machine" was likely to hold together and when it would not. Elkin and Stone observed that local politics are deceptively complex and that local politicians and business leaders do not always have coincidental interests. Consequently, major policy initiatives will normally be quite dif-

---

[2] Although, as Peterson claims, disputes over allocational policies often make up the heart of political conflicts in urban areas.

ficult to sustain. The key to successful policymaking is the ability of certain groups to coalesce into a governing "regime" that is able to formulate, enact, and carry through with complicated public policy. At the center of this regime model are social networks, the informal yet stable linkages among various political groups. Over time and through various acts of reciprocity, the component parts of a governing regime gain trust with each other and are willing to back one another's policy initiatives. Stone observed various periods in Atlanta's history during which commercial property holders or economic elites were able to accomplish their goals only when they build meaningful coalitions with leaders of the African American community.

Together, these works are at the heart of contemporary scholarly accounts of local politics and, when coupled with research on networks of political patronage and ethnic politics, they provide a very powerful mechanism for understanding the political dynamics of American big cities. Importantly, they also address many of the core issues of power and governance in American society. Collectively, these works set forth a picture of local politics that is less situated around the broad concerns of a democratic public but around the narrow and specific concerns of a small group with very concentrated interests. In other words, if all towns, villages, and boroughs were governed like big cities, then we would have good reason to believe that local politics are universally dominated by coalitions organized around maximizing returns on property investments, specific groups viewing local politics through the prism of race or ethnicity, and machine politicians holding office through patronage. Applying these models in such a universal way, one would inevitably conclude that decisions about how public revenues are generated and how public resources are distributed at the local level are motivated largely by the organizational clout of a small number of major property holders and not the average citizen. Such a situation does not speak well of the democratic potential of local government in America.

But this rather dark vision of local politics hinges on whether these theories can be generalized to all American localities—and, upon reflection, their portability appears quite limited. While theories of urban politics crafted over the past fifty years may provide a very good account of the governance of large cities, they do not provide a comprehensive account of *local* politics in general. In fact, as a group, these theories seem limited to a very specific class of urban place, big cities. Consider just a few problematic examples when trying to use them for small places. In many American towns and villages, it is probably impossible to identify a dominant economic elite, particularly if there are no large businesses or employers within their borders or everyone is of the same social class. Similarly, in many American municipalities, there are few commercial properties and opportunities for property speculation are quite limited; indeed, many affluent communities actively work to inhibit economic development in order to preserve the character of their towns. Nor do these theories offer any particular insight into the politics of school districts, other special district governments, or most small-scale democracies.

This is not to suggest that the studies cited are deficient; as descriptions of the politics in large cities, they provide invaluable insights. But currently, we have no way of knowing how widely applicable to local politics their models should be. Do they apply equally to a city of 25,000 as a city of 250,000? And, if not, what other factors then come to define local politics? Can they account for the politics of a mosquito abatement district as well as a small municipality?

As with other questions about comparative electoral local politics, a good way to answer these questions is to return to the framework utilized throughout this book and differentiate the places upon which these theories were created (i.e., large cities), from the vast majority of American municipalities. Looking at local politics this way, it appears that it is precisely the combination of larger size, relatively greater scope, and higher bias that gives urban politics the characteristics so often ascribed to it in the previous research. Consider, for example, the particular recipe for political success that Clarence Stone describes, namely the building of a political regime among leaders of key interest groups. Regime theory is mostly relevant to big cities because these are the only localities that combine a large population size with a moderate level of institutional scope and high level of bias, the very conditions that also sustain long-standing and conflicting political interests. When cities become so large, they require mass political mobilization and candidates will have to campaign by appealing to particular interest groups that can mobilize their supporters. When cities make major infrastructure improvements or provide great tax incentives for businesses, then there will be major property speculators seeking to shape local politics. And, when cities are under pressure to set aside a certain percentage of city jobs and contracts for particular groups, then stakeholders will emerge as vested political interests.

However, as one turns attention away from large cities and focuses on smaller places, the applicability of these same theories will increasingly depend on the places' relative scope and bias. Although the electoral politics of a town of 5,000 will be much more personal and intimate than those of a city of 5 million, their comparative political dynamics will be influenced more by the powers invested in their governing institutions and the amount of bias in their resource provisions. Elections in a large city with a limited scope, like Garland, Texas (population 222,000), will typically hinge more on issues of managerial competence. When a town is constricted to providing just a few municipal services and most decisions are handled by a professional city manager, there are significantly fewer opportunities for growth machines or elites to exercise any social or political prerogatives. Conversely, in a small community with a high degree of bias, like Hoboken, New Jersey or Bell, California, politics will be dominated by the same types of patronage or ethnic claims to resources that would be familiar to any observer of large cities. In these situations, it is very likely that politics will be dominated by a political regime oriented around an agenda of preserving the mal-apportionment of public resources.

That noted, the vast majority of American municipalities, special districts, and other smaller democracies simply are not high enough in either scope or bias to stimulate deep-seated or sustained conflict over public resources. As a result, few of the theories about local politics mentioned in this chapter are going to offer much insight into their affairs. For instance, political regimes are necessary only when there are ongoing conflicts over the priorities for government action; if government services are few and resources are uniformly distributed, most voters will have very similar preferences and the construction of political coalitions will simply be unnecessary. In most American cities, as in most managerial democracies, politics revolve around basic "custodial" issues related to service delivery and revenue concerns (Lewis and Neiman 2009). Most citizens should accept an equilibrium point between a certain level of taxes and service provision (Berry 2009). If they are all getting roughly similar levels of service and paying proportionately similar levels of taxes and fees, it is unlikely citizens will constantly agitate to change local politics. As long as local politicians adhere to this norm, local politics should remain relatively tranquil: political conflicts will be minor, elections will often be uncontested, and incumbents will do well at getting reelected.

As noted earlier, sharp fights will punctuate this political tranquility on occasion over substantive issues, but because these issues are typically temporal and parochial, it is very difficult to know when or where they will emerge. Like tornado strikes, the politics of managerial democracy, vacillating between periods of general calm and brief tumult, are hard to describe with a general theory of politics simply because the precise periods of tumult are so unpredictable. Just as we know the general conditions of when tornados are likely to hit, we might anticipate general conditions where incumbents are more likely to lose, but knowing where and when tornados hit or incumbents lose is going to be extremely hard to specify with any accuracy.

The unpredictability in politics is partly attributable to the general randomness of both natural and human affairs. Who can say when an earthquake, fire, or other unforeseen disaster will strike and cost a municipality millions? Who knows when the overheard off-color joke or comment is likely to be recorded and publicized? What determines whether an indignant constituent goes beyond simply voicing a complaint and decides to mount a political campaign? While a mayor or city council member can expect that any decision to raise taxes, lay off municipal employees, or cut services will be unpopular, he or she can never really know when or why such a decision will stimulate an organized political opposition that will generate a strong political opponent. Sometimes such measures will and sometimes they won't, and much of this depends on the skills, initiative, and personality of citizens willing to challenge the existing leadership. The great irony of managerial democracy is that the general stability that comes from a long-standing equilibrium between taxes and services leaves little room for predicting when points of disequilibrium ignite political opposition.

In sum, the dominant theories of local politics that were developed in regard to urban areas are not universally applicable to the vast majority of American municipalities. Most Americans live in managerial democracies, at least at the municipal level, or under a myriad of special district governments that may or may not have conditions that mimic the interest group politics of large cities. By identifying the differences in size, scope, and bias among these places, we can appreciate this fact and begin to reassess the consequences of these differences for democratic governance. However, before examining what managerial democracy means for the question of "who governs" America, we need to consider the second major body of scholarship on participatory democracy.

MANAGERIAL AND PARTICIPATORY DEMOCRACIES

In addition to their concerns with community power, political scholars have also made a host of assertions about the civic virtues of local governance. From the early commentaries of Alexis de Tocqueville to twentieth-century political theorists like John Dewey, Hannah Arendt, Carol Pateman, and Benjamin Barber, numerous theorists have viewed local politics not just as an arena of competition between elites and other groups, but as the best venue for citizens to empower themselves and fully realize democracy's transcendent possibilities. For these thinkers, the politics of small-scale democracy are not simply about identifying "who governs?" but are about what happens when citizens govern themselves in a localized way. These benefits are seen to come in two forms.

The first is the transformative capacities of civic involvement. This view originated with Alexis de Tocqueville's famous claim that citizen participation in local politics is essential for a well-functioning democracy because of its revelatory impact on the participant. By taking part in local democracy, citizens gain a "self-interest rightly understood," an uplifting view that allows the person to equate his or her own interests with that of the community. The Tocquevillian appreciation of local democracy has been taken up by later theorists, most notably by Benjamin Barber in his model of "strong democracy." Barber suggests that a purely representative democracy that exists in most liberal states extinguishes the range of possibilities available to citizens for realizing their true interests vis-à-vis their neighbors. Although Barber is concerned that ordinary civic participation in local government, "to the extent they are privatistic, or parochial or particularistic, will undermine democracy" (1983: 235), he nevertheless advocates a model of local engagement and deliberation that creates a more cosmopolitan sensibility among participants and builds a stronger basis of community among citizens. "Politics becomes its own university," Barber claims, "citizenship its own training ground, and participation its own tutor." (p. 152)

Local politics is also viewed as a bulwark against the large, impersonal politics of mass democracy at the state or national level and against the even more alienating practices of a neoliberal economic order. This strand of research goes back over a century to long-standing political concerns that ordinary citizens have little power within democratic systems to "actively play a role in shaping public decisions that affect their lives." (Gunn and Gunn 1991: 150). This grassroots movement started with progressive attempts at reforming local governments in the early twentieth century and became particularly strong in the 1960s and 1970s regarding community development corporations and the local implementation of federal and state policy initiatives (Berry, Portney, and Thomson 1993). When poor and disadvantaged citizens can become active participants in governing decisions, the thinking goes, they will make all levels of American government more meaningful and responsive to the concerns of constituents who are usually underrepresented in the political process (Hajnal 2007).

Although these perspectives enjoy a wide audience both in and out of the academy, it is unclear how germane they are in a contemporary American setting. Take the Tocquevillian argument that civic participation in local government fosters a "self-interest rightly understood." On the one hand, citizens who involve themselves in local government, particularly the ones who run for local office, seem to exemplify the Tocquevillian ideal. Given the limited extrinsic rewards of holding public office relative to the significant costs of seeking it, local politicians must be motivated by some intrinsic goals. And, as reported in chapter 3, most of them identify a feeling of civic duty as a primary motivating factor. Similarly, it is likely that most local voters are also driven to participate not simply from concerns over sustaining their property values, but also from attachments to a particular vision of their community, which would partly explain why long-term residents and citizens with greater interest in local affairs are so much more likely to vote.

On the other hand, the data do not allow us to draw any conclusions about whether it is their civic participation that fosters their stronger identification with their communities or the other way around. This distinction is vitally important because it speaks to the very high civic demands that come from a fragmented and decentralized democratic system in the United States. Unlike most industrialized democracies, American citizens are asked to participate in not just national and state governments, but county, municipal, and, increasingly, scores of special district governments as well. Combine these with the innumerable nongovernmental democracies comprised by America's civic sector, one could easily conclude that not only is participating in some kind of democratic activity almost impossible for any citizen to avoid, but that most citizens regularly face a barrage of democratic responsibilities. This is confirmed by survey data that indicate a comparatively high rate of American participation in local civic activities and voluntary associations (Almond and Verba 1963; Curtis, Baer, and Grabb 2001). But while there is abundant evidence that citizens who are active in local affairs are much more likely to trust their neighbors and identify with their communities (Howard and Gilbert 2008), there is still no empirical research that has been able to demonstrate a causal relationship (Oliver 2001; Van der Meer and Van Ingen 2008). We simply have no proof that participation in local politics makes citizens any more broad-minded or any more cosmopolitan in their political orientations.

Beyond the lack of evidence, this book's conceptual framework gives further reason to be skeptical of the transformative potential of local civic participation. As noted in chapter 2, citizen participation in civic affairs is directly related to the size, scope, and bias of a democracy. Civic participation is often higher in smaller democracies because of the higher degree of interpersonal contact among its members and candidates. In this regard, smaller democracies, by fostering political communities with a higher degree of interpersonal familiarity, may foster higher bonds of trust and mutual identification. Then again, they may stimulate greater personal animosity as well. Furthermore, democracies that are limited in scope provide fewer incentives for active participation because the range of contestable political issues is so narrow. And, in high-biased democracies, the incentives to participation come less from commitments to the democracy writ large than to contesting the inequitable distribution of its resources.

Together, these factors should give us pause when considering the factors that motivate citizen action. The history of American cities demonstrates that the effectiveness of participatory democracy hinges on the political mobilization of resource bias. Seemingly "nondemocratic" organizations like political machines arguably have been more effective mechanisms for empowering marginalized groups because they are able to sustain their participation through material compensation. Conversely, voluntary organizations and community development groups that advocate for public-use goods on behalf of marginalized citizens are going to be disadvantaged by their inability to sustain long-term involvement of the very groups they champion (Berry et al. 1993). In practice, local civic participation is driven by a myriad of different incentives, many of which may be in direct opposition to the greater good of a community.

It is also unclear whether participatory democracy can further the material interests of citizens, particularly those in marginalized communities. Despite their normative allure, most empirical tests about the impact of a "participatory" model of democracy have yielded at best mixed evidence on whether involving marginalized citizens actually can change the tenor of local politics. For example, in their in-depth study of community-based organizations in five cities, Berry et al. (1993) find little evidence that these groups meaningfully changed the agenda of city politics or furthered the ability of low-income citizens to involve themselves in the political process. Other research shows that government performance actually decreases with greater citizen control. Jeff Tessin (2009) finds that the performance of fire departments, state-prisons, and sewage systems are all worse in situations where citizens have greater control via direct democracy over governance.

Once again, part of the discrepancy may be understood relative to the size, scope, and bias of the democracy in question. Most theorizing and research on the putative benefits of participatory democracy focus on community groups in large urban areas, particularly in relation to the concerns of poor and minority citizens (Berry et al. 1993; Gunn and Gunn 1994). Yet, as discussed earlier, because of their greater size, particular scope, and high bias, large cities provide a distinctive type of political context for citizen action: not only are politicians and decision-makers more removed from constituents, political conflict is more likely to be organized and motivated by the specific interests of various stakeholders who are beneficiaries of biased government provision. Moreover, the constrained scope of big cities also means they have fewer and weaker political mechanisms available to address issues of social inequity. Although cities typically have more social programs than smaller places, they are still greatly limited in their capacities to redistribute resources to poor groups—most social programs in urban areas are largely financed with federal money.

With all the attention to grassroots democracy in big cities, few scholars have examined how America's suburbanization has influenced the potency of local civic action. Although large cities continue to hold disproportionately large numbers of minorities and low-income residents, the past forty years have seen a large influx of these groups into smaller jurisdictions within metropolitan areas. This migration would seem to hold mixed implications for participatory democracy. On the one hand, the American migration to smaller jurisdictions would make local leaders more available and presumably accountable to citizen concerns. It is much easier for a poor citizen to be heard by a local official in a town of 500 than a city of 5 million. On the other hand, smaller towns are even more limited in scope than large cities and are even less likely to hold programs that could address social problems. Furthermore, this higher degree of political fragmentation creates a competitive dynamic among various municipalities that puts downward pressure on redistribution of public goods (Peterson 1981). In other words, poor citizens may have limited political options in smaller places not just because their governments do less, but because their governments are constrained by geographic circumstance and fiscal competition with other localities.

In sum, it is not just the studies of urban politics that are limited in their applicability; theories of local civic participation also are inappropriate for most localities and have questionable empirical validity. Not only is it unlikely that most Americans are experiencing some Tocquevillian transformation as the consequence of their local civic participation, but there are also good reasons for doubting whether increased local activism will be an effective mechanism for marginalized groups to empower themselves in relation to an increasingly globalized, neoliberal economic order. Quite simply, the vision of local democracy conjured by political theorists is both inaccurate and applicable only to an increasingly small number of places that are far different than the places where most Americans reside.

RETHINKING LOCAL DEMOCRACY

So if the dominant theories of urban politics and participatory democracy are, at best, only applicable to a small portion of America's
localities, then how should we think about issues of "community
power" in contemporary America? Who really governs in a country where most citizens live in a place that could be described as
a managerial democracy? Although the sheer magnitude of these
questions defies any simple response, the framework of size, scope,
and bias can be useful in determining an answer. By examining the
implications of the mass migration of Americans over the past fifty
years to suburban municipalities that are smaller in size, more limited in scope, and less biased, we can begin to assess any imbalances in power and identify possible constraints on meaningful self-
governance. In short, with this simple framework, we can begin to
assess what the return to "small-town" government that epitomizes
America's suburbanization holds for American democracy.

Let us start with the political implications of small population
size. At the time the community power debates began, most Americans were either crowded in large cities or lived in sparsely populated rural areas: in 1950, over 36 percent resided in large, densely
populated cities while close to 40 percent lived in rural areas. By
many accounts, the large percentage of Americans in big cities was
disempowering for their capacities for self-governance; most accounts of the corruption, patronage, and alienation of city government inevitably mention the sheer size and scale of politics in
big cities as a problem for local democracy (e.g., Dahl 1961). But
over the past sixty years, a remarkable geographic transformation
has taken place in the United States. As noted earlier, today under
20 percent of Americans live in rural areas and only 25 percent
live in large cities over 100,000 in size; the majority of Americans
now live in small- to medium-sized towns, villages, and boroughs
within large metropolitan areas, places we commonly refer to as
suburbs. Thus the first task in assessing whether the managerial
character of most American municipalities is good for democracy
is to determine if this migration to smaller places has been empowering or disempowering for the American population.

Looking at changing population size alone, the evidence from this book and from past research indicates that moving one's population to smaller, subnational governing units is generally good. Not only are citizens in smaller places more likely to vote, but they are also more personally familiar with candidates, more attuned to issues, and generally more interested in public affairs (Oliver 2001). So to whatever extent a managerial democracy hinges on having a small constituency, we could say the predominance of Americans living in smaller municipalities should be empowering them in their capacities for self-governance.

Many scholars, however, view the migration to these smaller communities as an explicitly political act. The primary motivation for suburban political incorporation in the late nineteenth century was to inhibit annexation of residential areas to large urban centers. Beyond desires for preserving neighborhood autonomy, this resistance to political incorporation was an expression of latent racial, ethnic, and class tensions between middle-class, white suburbanites and poor, urban minorities (Jackson 1987). As state governments made incorporation easier, and as county and special district governments began providing more basic services, such as sewage, water, and fire protection, residential developments became increasingly empowered to resist being incorporated into nearby large cities and provided the framework for the patchwork of municipalities that are comprised by most American metropolitan areas today. In short, the movement to smaller places was itself partly an expression of race and class politics.

To understand the political implications of suburbanization, it is important to examine not just size but also the other factors of scope and bias. As noted throughout this book, most American municipalities are quite limited in their scope, particularly if they are small in size and surrounded by other municipalities. The range of governmental activities is not only explicitly limited by state laws and their city charters, they are also constrained by circumstances, or rather, their competition with other nearby municipalities for tax ratable (Peterson 1981; Teibout 1956). Thus most American towns and small cities concern themselves with issues pertaining to land use and local economic development, and typically provide only a handful of municipal services. Although a few smaller places provide a wider range of social services, such as housing, job training, and care for the elderly, the dominant trend among American suburban municipalities is toward limiting their services, particularly as the number and range of special district governments begins to increase (Berry 2009). When this is coupled with the prevalence of reform-style political institutions, such as council-manager governments that further divest power from a strong executive, it is clear that the typical American municipality, by itself, is a rather narrow and limited political institution.

Answering whether the restricted scope of most managerial democracies is any more or less empowering for the average American citizen probably depends largely both on one's political ideology and one's attitudes about local government.[3] For those who think local governments can be effective mechanisms for redressing social inequities, then the limited scope of a managerial democracy is undoubtedly a point of frustration. One may "think globally, act locally" as the popular bumper-sticker suggests, but without any meaningful ability to control the flow of capital or the conditions of labor, local governments are going to be a political instrument with a very limited range of applications. Conversely, for those who believe that local government is a vehicle for parochial corruption, then limiting the scope of local government may be an optimal configuration. Or, if one believes "that which governs best, governs least," then narrow range of local government service provision may be the best expression of democracy.

These issues of democratic accountability and responsiveness become even murkier when the characteristic of bias is considered.

---

[3] Most Americans seem to have contradictory views of local government. On the one hand, most Americans view local government positively, particularly in comparison with national or state institutions: a 2010 CNN poll found that 52 percent of Americans reported trusting local government "most or all" of the time, compared to only 26 percent who felt that way about the federal government. And, as mentioned above, political activists often argue that local government is a more authentic way to empower people and truly realize democratic values. On the other hand, Americans have a long history of being distrustful of seemingly all political institutions and efforts to limit the power of local governments that goes back well into the early nineteenth century. In many places, local governments are rightly viewed as being rife with corruption, incompetence, or favoritism.

As noted in previous chapters, bias is the most conceptually challenging dimension in this framework because it can take so many different forms and it is so endogenous to the political process. *All* governments inevitably contain some elements of bias and the extent of bias can vary dramatically depending on current officeholders. A highly unbiased town can suddenly become very biased if its political leaders decide to start redirecting government spending to a specific constituency or by deciding to hire people from only one group. And some towns, simply by virtue of their poverty or racial heterogeneity, are going to be more biased than others.

That noted, most small municipalities, as general-purpose governments, are relatively unbiased, particularly compared to large cities, states, and the federal government. Not only does their limited scope restrict their ability to be biased but also the particular types of services that most municipalities provide (e.g., fire and police protection, parks, libraries, water, sewage treatment) do not readily lend themselves to grossly differential applications across the population. Furthermore, most incumbents in a managerial democracy are probably unlikely to introduce a large amount of bias simply because any disruption to the equilibrium between taxes and services that most local voters use to evaluate incumbents might provoke some opposition. Indeed, when local political leaders do introduce bias into governing procedures, they will probably do so in an incremental way that is advertised only to the beneficiaries.

So does the unbiased character of most American municipalities mean that they are providing a better democracy than their biased state and federal counterparts? On one level, an unbiased government would seem to embody the basic democratic principles of equal treatment before the law. After all, what could be more democratic than a government that provides an equal level of services and resources? A town that gives every resident an equal level of police and fire protection and allows all citizens to visit parks and libraries would epitomize the classic democratic ideal.

Yet some may argue that for a government to be truly democratic, it needs to do more than treat all citizens the same; it actually needs to be biased in favor of disempowered groups (e.g.,

Piven and Cloward 1979). For those in dire poverty or who face racial or gender discrimination, equal treatment before the law is simply insufficient, according to this perspective, for ensuring equal access to self-governance. If a person is without food, shelter, or other basic necessities or if a person is subjected to systematic mistreatment because of his or her sex, race, or some other characteristic, then any notion of equality of service provision is relatively meaningless. A "level playing field" works only if everyone has access to it and chronic poverty or discrimination inhibits such action. It is this very logic that underlies many of the arguments for government programs like affirmative action, food stamps, or public housing.

Of course, whether or not government in an economically and racially stratified society needs to be biased in favor of marginalized groups in order to be more democratic is not only open to debate but involves a very complicated range of considerations, such as how one determines the extent of a group's marginalization or what government can or needs to do in order to redress it. Many opponents of affirmative action programs in government hiring and contracting, for example, often claim that not only are such programs ineffectual in redressing America's long history of racial discrimination against African Americans but, given nearly fifty years since the passage of the Civil Rights Act, such programs are no longer necessary (Sowell 2004). These problems are further compounded given the limited capacities of local government to redistribute wealth in any systematic manner (Peterson 1981). In other words, even if local democracies do seek to institute biased allocations of their resources to promote social justice, they are statutorily and circumstantially constrained in their capacities to do so.

Another critique of the seemingly low bias in most American municipalities also relates to this nation's increasing suburbanization. According to some historians (Jackson 1987), the unbiased character of most American governments is not merely accidental, but the direct consequence of white middle- and upper-class groups seeking to protect certain race and class prerogatives through suburban municipal segregation. As many white Americans moved

to the suburbs, they not only sought to politically distance themselves from racial and ethnic minorities in large cities, but they
also sorted themselves (or were sorted by a differentiated housing
market) along class lines. This migration institutionalized patterns
of geographic segregation that had occurred in large cities. With
suburbanization, what were once rich, middle-class, working, and
poor *neighborhoods* in one city became rich, middle-class, working, and poor *municipalities* in one metropolitan area.

As middle- and upper-class Americans segregated themselves
into more socially and economically homogeneous places, it becomes easier to sustain an unbiased government because they
shared a more uniform set of political preferences with their neighbors. When all residents demand similar levels of government services or have to pay similar levels of taxes, government services
can be delivered in a relatively consistent manner without a great
deal of political contestation. In short, smaller, suburban governments could be less biased because they hosted a narrower range
of political interests and fewer groups making conflicting political
demands.

But a low level of bias in any one individual community may
mask a larger, more systematic amount of bias across an entire
metropolitan area. Residents of a solely middle-class or wealthy
suburb may enjoy relatively lower property taxes than residents
of a nearby poor suburb even if they are getting the same level of
services. A $2 million annual budget for a fire department will be
comparatively more costly for residents of a poor community of
5,000 people than in a wealthy community of the same size. When
citizens fund and receive local services at the municipal level, and
when municipal boundaries divide citizens by class and race, large
discrepancies in the quality of public services are likely to emerge,
particularly in the absence of state or federal redistribution.

In sum, while the characteristic of size, scope, and bias do not
provide any definitive answers to the question of "who governs"
America, they do provide a useful framework for understanding
the dynamics of power and politics at the local level. These might
not tell us whether economic elites, property speculators, or coalitions of various interests govern in any particular place, but they

can give us an idea about the types of places where certain types of politics and power relations are likely to occur. They also give us some tools for understanding the political implications of America's suburbanization. Although this does not lead to any simple generalizations about community power in suburban America, we can appreciate how the migration to smaller, more homogeneous municipalities creates a distinct set of trade-offs between government accountability and higher discrepancies in the quality of local government services. How one weighs these trade-offs and evaluates their implications for democracy will depend on one's view about the role of government in society and the obligations of the state for ensuring greater social equality.

FINAL THOUGHTS

Like any new area of research, this inquiry into local elections probably raises more questions than it answers. It certainly leaves many aspects of local elections unexamined. For instance, we did not explore the full range of local electoral contests, such as recall elections, bond measures, or even elections for city clerks, library or school boards, and many other local offices. We did not examine what drives voters in elections for open seats to mayoral or city council positions. We did not examine the impact of factors that professionals claim are important for winning local contests, such as yard signs, canvassing, newspaper ads, or other campaign techniques. And, most noticeably, this book did not compare local elections to the other types of democracies that vary in regards to size, scope, and bias.

For many readers, this final omission may be the most frustrating. After spelling out an elaborate framework for differentiating democracies in chapter 1, the rest of the book ended up focusing most of its attention on just one cell. Despite a few oblique references to studies of presidential elections, we did not really compare municipal elections to special district, school board, county, or state elections. These are democracies that are generally greater in size and scope and often higher in bias than most municipalities.

Any reader would be right to wonder just how much elections do vary along different points of each dimension as the earlier deductions would claim. We do too.

But despite the grandiosity of its theory, the intention of this book was primarily to explain local municipal elections and, in order to do this, we needed to first differentiate them from national ones. We hope the theoretical framework offered was insightful in showing how local races are categorically different than larger ones. And we hope our readers accept this book as more of a first step than a final word. Given the paucity of research on local elections, particularly in the suburban places where most Americans live, we have tried to provide some conceptual tools for understanding this largely unexamined aspect of American democracy. And just as we have been greatly assisted by the research efforts of those cited throughout this book, we hope that the various insights we gained from attempting to conceptualize how elections work in small localities will be useful for those who wish to further explore all of these areas we left unexamined.

References

Aldrich, John H., John L. Sullivan, and Eugene Borgida. 1989. "Foreign Affairs and Issue Voting: Do Presidential Candidates Waltz Before a Blind Audience?" *American Political Science Review* 83(1): 123–41.

Almond, Gabriel A., and Sidney Verba. 1963. *The Civic Culture: Political Attitudes and Democracy in Five Nations.* Princeton: Princeton University Press.

Alesina, Alberto, Reza Baqir, and William Easterly. 1999. "Public Goods and Ethnic Divisions." *Quarterly Journal of Economics* 114(4): 1254–73.

Alesina, Alberto, and Enrico Spoalare. 2003. *The Size of Nations.* Cambridge: MIT Press.

Alvarez, R. Michael, and Jonathan Nagler. 1998. "Economic Entitlements and Social Issues: Voter Choice in the 1998 Presidential Election." *American Journal of Political Science* 42(4): 1349–63.

Ansolabehere, Stephen, and Jame M. Snyder. 2002. "The Incumbency Advantage in U.S. Elections: An Analysis of State and Federal Offices, 1942–2000." *Election Law Journal* 1(3): 315–38.

Ansolabehere, Stephen, Rebecca Lessem, and James M. Snyder. 2006. "The Orientation of Newspaper Endorsements in U.S. Elections, 1940–2002." *Quarterly Journal of Political Science* 1: 393–404.

Ansolabehere, Stephen, Jonathan Rodden, and James M. Snyder. 2008. "The Strength of Issues: Using Multiple Measures to Gauge Preference Stability, Ideological Constraints, and Issue Voting." *American Political Science Review* 102(2): 215–32.

Anzia, Sarah. 2011. "Electoral Timing and the Electoral Influence of Interest Groups." *Journal of Politics.* Forthcoming.

Arnold, Douglas. 1992. *The Logic of Congressional Action.* New Haven: Yale University Press.

Banfield, Edward C., and James Q. Wilson. 1963. *City Politics.* Cambridge: Harvard University Press.

Barber, Benjamin R. 1983. *Strong Democracy: Participatory Politics for a New Age.* Berkeley: University of California Press.

Bartels, Larry M. 1996. "Uninformed Votes: Information Effects in Presidential Elections." *American Journal of Political Science* 40(1): 194–230.

———. 2002. "Beyond the Running Tally: Partisan Bias in Political Perception." *Political Behavior* 24(2): 117–50.

———. 2008. *Unequal Democracy: The Political Economy of the New Gilded Age.* Princeton: Princeton University Press.

Berry, Christopher R. 2009. *Imperfect Union: Representation and Taxation in Multilevel Governments.* New York: Cambridge University Press.

Berry, Christopher R., and William G. Howell. 2007. "Accountability and Local Elections: Rethinking Retrospective Voting." *Journal of Politics* 69(3): 844–58.

Berry, Jeffrey M., Kent E. Portney, and Ken Thomson. 1993. *The Rebirth of Urban Democracy.* Washington, D.C.: Brookings Institution.

Bridges, Amy. 1997. *Morning Glories: Municipal Reform in the Southwest.* Princeton: Princeton University Press.

Browning, Rufus P., Dale Rogers Marshall, and David H. Tabb. 2003. *Racial Politics in American Cities.* 3rd edition. New York: Longman.

Campbell, Andrea L. 2005. *How Policies Make Citizens: Senior Political Activism and the American Welfare State.* Princeton: Princeton University Press.

Campbell, Angus, Philip E. Converse, Warren E. Miller, and Donald E. Stokes. 1960. *The American Voter.* Chicago: University of Chicago Press.

Campbell, David E. 2009. "Civic Engagement and Education: An Empirical Test of the Sorting Model." *American Journal of Political Science* 53(4): 771–86.

Carmines, Edward G., and James A. Stimson. 1980. "The Two Faces of Issue Voting." *American Political Science Review* 74(1): 78–91.

Citrin, Jack, Eric Schickler, and John Sides. 2003. "What If Everyone Voted? Simulating the Impact of Increased Turnout in Senate Elections." *American Journal of Political Science* 47(1): 75–90.

Converse, Philip E. 1964. "The Nature of Belief Systems in Mass Publics." In *Ideology and Discontent*, edited by David E. Apter. Glencoe, Ill.: Free Press.

Curtis, James E., Douglas E. Baer, and Edward G. Grabb. 2001. "Nations of Joiners: Explaining Voluntary Association Membership in Democratic Societies." *American Sociological Review* 66(6): 783–805.

Dahl, Robert A. 1961. *Who Governs? Democracy and Power in an American City.* New Haven: Yale University Press.

———. 2000. *On Democracy.* New Haven: Yale University Press.

Dahl, Robert A., and Edward R. Tufte. 1973. *Size and Democracy.* Palo Alto: Stanford University Press.

Dee, Thomas S. 2004. "Are There Civic Returns to Education?" *Journal of Public Economics* 88(9–10): 1697–20.

Delli Carpini, Michael X., and Scott Keeter. 1997. *What Americans Know About Politics and Why It Matters.* New Haven: Yale University Press.

Downs, Anthony. 1957. *An Economic Theory of Democracy.* New York: Harper.

Ehrenhalt, Alan. 1992. *The Lost City: The Forgotten Virtues of Community in America.* New York: Basic Books.

Elkin, Stephen L. 1987. *City and Regime in American Public.* Chicago: University of Chicago Press.

Erie, Stephen P. 1988. *Rainbow's End: Irish-Americans and the Dilemmas of Urban Machine Politics, 1840–1985.* Berkeley: University of California Press.

Fiorina, Morris P. 1981. *Retrospective Voting in American National Elections.* New Haven: Yale University Press.

Fischel, William A. 2005. *The Homevoter Hypothesis: How Home Values Influence Local Government Taxation, School Finance, and Land-Use Policies.* Cambridge: Harvard University Press.

Frank, Thomas. 2004. *What's the Matter with Kansas? How Conservatives Won the Heart of America.* New York: Henry Holt.

Franklin, Mark N. 2004. *Voter Turnout and the Dynamics of Electoral Competition in Established Democracies since 1945.* New York: Cambridge University Press.

Fuchs, Ester R. 1992. *Mayors and Money: Fiscal Policy in New York and Chicago.* Chicago: University of Chicago Press.

Gerber, Alan S., Donald P. Green, and Christopher W. Larimer. 2008. "Social Pressure and Voter Turnout: Evidence from a Large-Scale Field Experiment." *American Political Science Review* 102(1): 33–48.

Gilens, Martin. 2001. "Political Ignorance and Collective Policy Preferences." *American Political Science Review* 95(2): 379–96.

Green, Donald P., and Alan S. Gerber. 2008. *Get-Out-the-Vote: How to Increase Voter Turnout.* 2nd edition. Washington, D.C.: Brookings Institution.

Green, Donald P., Alan S. Gerber, and David W. Nickerson. 2003. "Getting Out the Vote in Local Elections: Results from Six Door-to-Door Canvassing Experiments." *Journal of Politics* 65(4): 1083–96.

Green, Donald P., Bradley Palmquist, and Eric Schickler. 2004. *Partisan Hearts and Minds: Political Parties and the Social Identities of Voters.* New Haven: Yale University Press.

Gunn, Christopher Eaton, and Hazel Dayton Gunn. 1991. *Reclaiming Capital: Democratic Initiatives and Community Development.* Ithaca: Cornell University Press.

Hacker, Jacob, and Paul Pierson. 2010. *Winner Take All Politics.* New York: Simon and Schuster.

Hajnal, Zoltan L. 2007. *Changing White Attitudes toward Black Political Leadership.* New York: Cambridge University Press.

Hajnal, Zoltan L., and Paul G. Lewis. 2003. "Municipal Institutions and Voter Turnout in Local Elections." *Urban Affairs Review* 38(5): 645–68.

Hajnal, Zoltan L., and Jessica Trounstine. 2005. "Where Turnout Matters: the Consequences of Uneven Turnout in City Politics." *Journal of Politics* 67(2): 515–35.

Hamilton, Alexander, James Madison, and John Jay. [1789] 1961. *The Federalist Papers.* New York: American New Library of World Literature.

Highton, Benjamin. 1997. "Easy Registration and Voter Turnout." *Journal of Politics* 59(2): 565–75.

Highton, Benjamin, and Raymond E. Wolfinger. 2001. "The Political Implication of Higher Turnout." *British Journal of Political Science* 31(1): 179–223.

Hillygus, D. Sunshine, and Todd G. Shields. 2008. *The Persuadable Voter: Wedge Issues in Presidential Campaigns.* Princeton: Princeton University Press.

Hirschman, Albert. 1970. *Exit, Voice, and Loyalty: Responses to Decline in Firms, Organizations, and States.* Cambridge: Harvard University Press.

Howard, Marc Morje, and Leah Gilbert. 2008. "A Cross-National Comparison of the Internal Effects of Participation in Voluntary Organizations." *Political Studies* 56(1): 12–32.

Howell, William G., ed. 2005. *Besieged: School Boards and the Future of Education Politics.* Washington, D.C.: Brookings Institution.

Hunter, Floyd. 1952. *Community Power Structure: A Study of Decision-Makers.* Chapel Hill: University of North Carolina Press.

Jackson, Kenneth T. 1987. *Crabgrass Frontier: The Suburbanization of the United States*. New York: Oxford University Press.

Jacobson, Gary C. 2008. *The Politics of Congressional Election*. 7th edition. New York: Longman.

Kaufman, Karen M. 2004. *The Urban Voter: Group Conflict and Mayoral Voting Behavior in New York and Los Angeles*. Ann Arbor: University of Michigan Press.

Key, V.O. 1966. *The Responsible Electorate: Rationality in Presidential Voting*. Cambridge: Belknap Press.

Kiewiet, D. Roderick, and Douglas Rivers. 1984. "A Retrospective on Retrospective Voting." *Political Behavior* 6(4): 369–93.

Kinder, Donald R., and D. Roderick Kiewiet. 1981. "Sociotropic Voting: The American Case." *British Journal of Political Science* 11(2): 129–61.

King, Gary, Michael Tomz, and Jason Wittenberg. 2000. "Making the Most of Statistical Analyses: Improving Interpretations and Presentation." *American Journal of Political Science* 44(2): 347–61.

Knoke, David. 1977. "The Political Structure of Rural America." *Annals of the American Academy of Political and Social Science* 429(1): 51–62.

Krebs, Timothy B. 1998. "The Determinants of Candidates' Vote Share and the Advantages of Incumbency in City Council Elections." *American Journal of Political Science* 42(3): 921–35.

Lee, Eugene C. 1960. *The Politics of Nonpartisanship: A Study of California City Elections*. Berkeley: University of California Press.

Lieske, Joel. 1989. "The Political Dynamics of Urban Voting Behavior." *American Journal of Political Science* 33:150–74.

Lewis-Beck, Michael, William Jacoby, Helmut Norpoth, and Herbert Weisberg. 2008. *The American Voter Revisited*. Ann Arbor: University of Michigan Press.

Lewis, Paul G., and Max Neiman. 2009. *Custodians of Place: Governing the Growth and Development of Cities*. Washington, D.C.: Georgetown University Press.

Lipjhart, Arend. 1999. *Patterns of Democracy*. New Haven: Yale University Press.

Logan, John R., and Harvey L. Molotch. 1987. *Urban Fortunes: The Political Economy of Place*. Berkeley: University of California Press.

Lowery, David, and William E. Lyons. 1989. "The Impact of Jurisdictional Boundaries: An Individual-Level Test of the Tiebout Model." *Journal of Politics* 51(1): 73–97.

Lowi, Theodore J. 1964. *At the Pleasure of the Mayor: Patronage and Power in New York City, 1898–1958*. Glencoe, Ill: Free Press.

Markus, Gregory B., and Philip E. Converse. 1979. "A Dynamic Simultaneous Equation Model of Electoral Choice." *American Political Science Review* 73(4): 1055–70.

Mauro, Paolo. 1998. "Corruption and the Composition of Government Expenditure." *Journal of Public Economics* 69(2): 263–79.

Mayhew, David R. 2004. *Congress: The Electoral Connection*. 2nd edition. New Haven: Yale University Press.

McCarty, Nolan, Keith T. Poole, and Howard Rosenthal. 2006. *Polarized America: The Dance of Ideology and Unequal Riches*. Cambridge: MIT Press.

McDonald, Michael P., and Samuel L. Popkin. 2001. "The Myth of the Vanishing Voter." *American Political Science Review* 95(4): 963–74.

Miller, Gary J. 1981. *Cities by Contract: The Politics of Municipal Incorporation.* Cambridge: MIT Press.

Mills, C. Wright. 1956. *The Power Elite.* New York: Oxford University Press.

Moe, Terry M. 2005. "Teacher Unions and School Board Elections." Pp. 254–87 in *Besieged: School Boards and the Future of Education Politics,* edited by William G. Howell. Washington, D.C.: Brookings Institute.

Mollenkopf, John H. 1983. *The Contested City.* Princeton: Princeton University Press.

Mondak, Jeffery J., Diana C. Mutz, and Robert Huckfeldt. 1996. "Persuasion in Context: The Multilevel Structure of Economic Evaluation." In *Political Persuasion and Attitude Change,* edited by Diana C. Mutz, Paul M. Sniderman, and Richard A. Brody. Ann Arbor: University of Michigan Press.

Nadeau, Richard, and Michael S. Lewis-Beck. 2001. "National Economic Voting in US Presidential Elections." *Journal of Politics* 63(1): 159–81.

Okediji, Tade. 2005. "The Dynamics of Ethnic Fragmentation: A Proposal for an Expanded Measurement Index." *American Journal of Economics and Sociology* 64 (2): 637–62.

Oliver, J. Eric. 2001. *Democracy in Suburbia.* Princeton: Princeton University Press.

Oliver, J. Eric, and Raymond E. Wolfinger. 1999. "Jury Aversion and Voter Registration." *American Political Science Review* 93(1): 147–52.

Olken, Benjamin. 2007. "Monitoring Corruption: Evidence from a Field Experiment in Indonesia." *Journal of Political Economy* 115(2): 200–219.

Olson, Mancur. 1965. *The Logic of Collective Action: Public Goods and the Theory of Groups.* Cambridge: Harvard University Press.

Pelton, Robert. 1990. *Loney Laws . . . That You Never Knew You Were Breaking.* New York: Walker & Co.

Peterson, Paul E. 1981. *City Limits.* Chicago: University of Chicago Press.

Piven, Frances Fox, and Richard A. Cloward. 1979. *Poor People's Movements: Why They Succeed, How They Fail.* New York: Vintage Books.

———. 2000. *Why Americans Still Don't Vote and Why Politicians Want It That Way.* Boston: Beacon Press.

Polsby, Nelson. 1980. *Community Power and Political Theory.* New Haven: Yale University Press.

Powell, G. Bingham. 1986. "American Voter Turnout in Comparative Perspectives." *American Political Science Review* 80(1): 17–43.

Powell, G. Bingham, and Guy Whitten. 1993. "A Cross-National Account of Economic Voting." *American Journal of Political Science* 37(2): 391–414.

Riker, William H., and Peter C. Ordeshook. 1968. "A Theory of Calculus of Voting." *American Political Science Review* 62(1): 25–42.

Rosenstone, Steven J., and John Mark Hansen. 1993. *Mobilization, Participation, and Democracy in America.* New York: MacMillan.

Shaw, Catherine. 2004. *The Campaign Manager: Running and Winning Local Elections.* 3rd edition. Boulder, Colo.: Westview Press.

Sowell, Thomas. 2004. *Affirmative Action around the World: An Empirical Study.* New Haven: Yale University Press.

Stein, Lana, and Arnold Fleischmann. 1987. "Newspaper and Business Endorsements in Municipal Elections: A Test of the Conventional Wisdom." *Journal of Urban Affairs* 9(4): 325–36.

Stone, Clarence N. 1989. *Regime Politics: Governing Atlanta, 1946–1988*. Lawrence: University Press of Kansas.

Teaford, Jon C. 1979. *City and Suburb: The Political Fragmentations of Metropolitan America, 1850–1970*. Baltimore: Johns Hopkins University Press.

Teske, Paul, Mark Schneider, Michael Mintrom, and Samuel Best. 1993. "Establishing the Microfoundations of a Macro Theory: Information, Movers, and the Competitive Local Market for Public Goods." *American Political Science Review* 87(3): 702–13.

Tessin, Jeff. 2009. "Representation and Government Performance." Ph.D. diss., Princeton University.

Tiebout, Charles M. 1956. "A Pure Theory of Local Expenditures." *Journal of Political Economy* 64(5): 416–24.

Tomz, Michael, and Robert Van Howling. 2009. "The Electoral Implications of Candidate Ambiguity." *American Political Science Review* 103(1): 83–98.

Tomz, Michael, Jason Wittenberg, and Gary King. 2003. *CLARIFY: Software for Interpreting and Presenting Statistical Results*. Version 2.1. Stanford University, University of Wisconsin, and Harvard University. January 5. Available at http://gking.harvard.edu/.

Trounstine, Jessica L. 2008. *Political Monopolies in American Cities: The Rise and Fall of Bosses and Reformers*. Chicago: University of Chicago Press.

Van der Meer, Tom, and Erik J. Van Ingen. 2008. "Schools of Democracy? Disentangling the Relationship between Civic Participation and Political Action in 17 European Countries." *European Journal of Political Research* 48(2): 281–308.

Verba, Sidney, Kay Lehman Schlozman, and Henry E. Brady. 1995. *Voice and Equality: Civic Voluntarism in American Politics*. Cambridge: Harvard University Press.

Wantchekon, Leonard. 2003. "Clientalism and Voting Behavior: Evidence from a Field Experiment in Benin." *World Politics* 55(3): 399–422.

Wattenberg, Martin P., Ian McAllister, and Anthony Salvanto. 2000. "How Voting Is Like Taking an SAT Test: An Analysis of American Voter Rolloff." *American Political Quarterly* 28: 234–50.

Wolfinger, Raymond E. 1974. "Why Political Machines Have Not Withered Away and Other Revisionist Thoughts." *Journal of Politics* 34(2): 365–88.

Wolfinger, Raymond E., and Steven J. Rosenstone. 1980. *Who Votes?* New Haven: Yale University Press.

Wood, Curtis. 2002. "Voter Turnout in City Elections." *Urban Affairs Review* 38(2): 209–31.

Zaller, John R. 2004. "Floating Voters in U.S. Presidential Elections, 1948–2000." In *Studies in Public Opinion: Attitudes, Nonattitudes, Measurement Error, and Change*, edited by Willem E. Saris and Paul M. Sniderman. Princeton: Princeton University Press.

Index